BOOKS BY RICHARD ARMOUR

Biography and Literary Criticism

Barry Cornwall: A Biography of Bryan Waller Procter
The Literary Recollections of Barry Cornwall
Coleridge the Talker (with Raymond F. Howes)

Play

To These Dark Steps (with Bown Adams)

Light Verse

An Armoury of Light Verse
For Partly Proud Parents
Golf Bawls
Leading with My Left
Light Armour
The Medical Muse
Nights with Armour
Privates' Lives
Punctured Poems
Yours for the Asking

Prose Humor and Satire

American Lit Relit
Armour's Almanac
The Classics Reclassified

A Diabolical Dictionary of Education
Drug Store Days
English Lit Relit
Going Around in Academic Circles
Going Like Sixty
Golf Is a Four-Letter Word
It All Started with Columbus
It All Started with Europa
It All Started with Eve
It All Started with Freshman English
It All Started with Hippocrates
It All Started with Marx
It All Started with Stones and Clubs
My Life with Women
Out of My Mind
A Safari into Satire
A Short History of Sex
Through Darkest Adolescence
Twisted Tales from Shakespeare
Writing Light Verse
Writing Light Verse and Prose Humor

For All Ages

All in Sport
The Strange Dreams of Rover Jones

For Children

The Adventures of Egbert the Easter Egg
All Sizes and Shapes of Monkeys and Apes
Animals on the Ceiling
A Dozen Dinosaurs
Odd Old Mammals
On Your Marks: A Package of Punctuation
Our Presidents
Who's in Holes?
The Year Santa Went Modern

GOING LIKE SIXTY

A LIGHTHEARTED LOOK AT THE LATER YEARS

Richard Armour

McGRAW-HILL BOOK COMPANY

New York   Toronto   St. Louis
Düsseldorf   Mexico   Panama

Book design by Marcy J. Katz

Library of Congress Cataloging in Publication Data

Armour, Richard Willard, 1906–
    Going like sixty.

    I. Title.
PS3501.R55G58   818'.5'207   73-13783
ISBN 0-07-002291-7

123456789 BPBP 7987654

Dedicated
to Father Time,
who is older than any of us.

Most of the verses scattered through the book first appeared in *Family Health, Family Weekly, Los Angeles Times, The New York Times, Quote, The Saturday Evening Post, Saturday Review,* and *The Wall Street Journal.* Permission to include this material in the present book is gratefully acknowledged.

Contents

1. Warming Up to the Subject   *1*
2. How Old Is Old?   *11*
3. Looking Forward To and Sideways At Retirement   23
4. And Now Where Shall We Live?   35
5. Taking Advantage of the Advantages   49
6. Getting Exercised About It   59
7. Sex and the Senior Citizen   69
8. Income and Outgo   77
9. The Company You Keep Keeps You Company   87
10. Getting Away from It All   97
11. Audio-Visual Matters   *107*
12. A Short Course in Medicine   *115*
13. Generating Generations   *127*

1.

Warming Up
to the Subject

Some years ago I wrote a book called *Through Darkest Adolescence.* Our children were then teenagers, and I found much of what they were going through interesting, even incredible. Some of their friends I found even more fascinating, though at times they were also a bit nauseating, and it was the clinical study of these acne-ridden creatures that probably led to my addiction to antacid tablets.

I wrote about adolescence as if it were a disease, which I still think it is, but a disease that virtually (if not virtuously) everyone gets. Now that our children have children whose adolescence they will have to cope with themselves, I am turning to another subject, something that is currently closer to me. If I am not an authority on it, at least I am intimately involved with it. Adolescence, which I once wrote about, now seems remote. But old age, which I herewith propose to explore, is upon me.

This leads me to quote some lines I wrote, it is hard to believe, when I was only sixty, called "Putting in My Or":

> "Oh, to be young and handsome!"
> I sigh, and yet more and more
> Instead of saying "young and"
> I find myself saying "young or."

But now that I have lived through more seasons and have become better seasoned, or more accustomed to my present custom, I actually like these later years, and to heck with how I look. I am less wistful, less choosy, and glad to be alive and reasonably well. As I write this, I am unreasonably well, which is better still.

Unlike adolescence, old age is not a disease, which is something you get and then with proper treatment get over. Old age—or elderliness or late middle age or maturity or senior citizenship or whatever you wish to call it—is something you simply get. It is not a phase, it is a culmination. It is as if something planted in the garden, after an onward and upward struggle from seed to shoot to plant, under constant attack by aphids, scale, ants, underwatering, overwatering, and all the rest, has at last put forth a flower.

It isn't those who have reached old age for whom I feel sorry, it is those who didn't quite make it. They missed something.

But let me take another tack, or possibly nail.

I have always wanted to begin a book with a Profound Statement, if possible an aphorism that would find its way into Bartlett's *Familiar Quotations*. So before I go further let me get this bit of profundity off my chest or off my back or wherever it has been. Here it is: *There is nothing new about old age*.

One thing that makes my statement so intriguing and memorable is that it is open to interpretation. Where would such as Aristotle, Shakespeare, and Faulkner be if their every phrase were so obvious that everything was understood about it at first reading? Professors, especially in graduate schools, would have nothing left to do. The learned journals, replete with scholarly interpretations and re-interpretations, would go out of business.

Without getting into the subtler and more esoteric interpretations of "There is nothing new about old age," I cannot wait to point out three possible meanings of this sage remark. First, it could mean that there is nothing new that can be said about old age. I reject this meaning at once and with considerable indignation. If this were true I could not or should not write this book.

Second, "There is nothing new about old age" could be telling us that there is no element of newness in old age. There are no surprises, no remarkable and unexpected happenings. This I also reject, since it is far more likely that something exciting can happen in old age, such as falling and breaking your hip, than in youth.

Finally, "There is nothing new about old age" could mean that old age has been with us since time immemorial, and even earlier. Consider Methuselah, who according to the Bible lived 969 years, which shows that there certainly must have been old age in those days, and lots of it. Even if the scholars, or spoilsports, are right, and Methuselah's longevity was exaggerated and he lived to be only eight hundred or so, he had more experience with old age than most people do today, even with Geritol and Vitamin E.

It is this third meaning of "There is nothing new about old age" that I had in mind when I conceived the idea. What I mean is that old age is nothing new, that it has been around a long time, that billions of people have experienced it, and that it is universal. There are instances of old age in New York City and in Cedar Rapids, in Afghanistan and in Ecuador. Old age itself is old.

Moreover, I have discovered that old age is a fascinating subject. In my circle, made up largely of squares, it is almost as good a topic of conversation as the weather and insomnia, though it may be necessary to repeat what you were saying if someone in the group shouts "What was that?" or "You'll have to speak a little louder."

Old people, I have discovered, take old age in different ways. Some accept it as inevitable and are tolerant of it. Some ignore it, pretending it isn't there. Some are aware of it, but only in others.

4

Some fight it, snarl at it, curse it. Still others, believe it or not, enjoy it.

One of our favorite indoor sports, requiring neither physical exertion nor much intellectual activity, is to sit around and ask one another "How old (or young) would you like to be if you could pick an age?"

"Oh, to be seventy again!" exclaimed a friend of mine who is eighty-two. He is a vigorous, virile type, with a lively sense of humor.

"I would like to be about fifty," said a woman who doesn't tell her age but I think is around seventy-three. (In fact I know she is, because I looked up when she graduated from college, a good way of figuring out such things.)

"I'd like to be thirty," said another, a man who wears clothes that are distinctly mod. He was the first of my friends to grow long sideburns and to pick up the current slang. I happen to know he is pushing seventy, in fact may have pushed past it. He not only would like to be thirty but apparently feels he *is* thirty, or even twenty-nine.

"I'd like to be anything but a teenager," one woman said firmly. "I couldn't go through it again, especially these days, with drugs and all the rest." She, I happen to know, is in her late seventies.

"I wouldn't want to be a year younger," still another said, a woman who is right around sixty-seven. "I'd hate to live my life all over. I might not do as well the next time."

None of my friends mentioned wishing to be twenty-one. This disappointed me, because I wanted to quote a piece of verse I wrote recently based on A. E. Housman's famous "When I was one-and-twenty." This is the way (not a very long way) it goes:

When I was one-and-twenty
I knew the answers well,
And anyone who listened
I'd very quickly tell.

I knew the right and wrong then,
The error of men's ways.
I never was mistaken
Back in those golden days.

I knew the world had problems;
They caused me, though, no fright.
For I, if just they asked me,
Could quickly set them right.

When I was one-and-twenty,
Impatient, restless, keen,
I was as sure, all-knowing
As those today eighteen.

A psychiatrist, or a specialist in geriatrics, might find these different reactions to age revealing. I learned a little from them myself, but would have learned more if I could have been sure each person was telling the truth.

As for myself, I find the answer complicated.

Being the greedy type, I want the perspective and accumulated knowledge of age and the physical attributes of youth. I want the memories of the past that come with age but I also want youth's prospect of a long future in which to accomplish certain things for myself and also to see what happens to my grandchildren and the world and the human race in the next half-century or so. Will they get rid of air pollution? Will they stop fighting wars? Will they discover life, especially something resembling human life, on distant planets?

Some of these things I may live to see, if they hurry up. Others I'm afraid I'll miss.

What I have learned so far about old age is that it is possible to do many more things than young people think you can. I can do (and I do them every morning) thirty full-fledged pushups without stopping, and no cheating. I thought this was pretty good until I watched a man ten years older than I do forty. I know there are elderly people (I use the word with some trepidation) who do a hundred pushups a day, but not all at once. What they tell you, though, is simply "I do a hundred pushups a day."

I could do six hundred pushups a day, and without breathing hard, if I did ten every ten minutes, sixty an hour, during a ten-hour day. At least I think I could, and one of these days I may try it.

As for sex, I shall have something to say about it in a subsequent chapter. But, not to keep you in suspense, let me make a few remarks here.

There are many books written by M.D.'s and sexologists that will tell you all you have ever wanted to know but were afraid to ask about sex after seventy. Whether you believe what they say in such books is a personal matter.

However, I do know a few things about sex in "the later years" myself. One is that it is later than it was earlier. But, as the old proverb has it, though probably in another context, "Better late than never." This, I might add, is contained in John Heywood's *Proverbs*, a very clean book first printed in 1546, one year before the death of King Henry VIII. Henry, who had six wives, lived only into his middle fifties, and there may have been some connection between his lack of longevity and his numerous spouses, though I doubt it.

Anyhow, if you need further encouragement and instruction, without being caught with one of those current sex manuals and being thought a dirty old man or dirty old woman, I suggest you carry around with you, or keep on your bedside table, a copy of Heywood's book. In it you will find such sage advice as "Strike while the iron is hot" and "Nothing is impossible to a willing heart." When his book of proverbs was printed, Heywood was forty-nine. However forty-nine in those days was like seventy-nine today, and Heywood undoubtedly still had sex on his mind and was optimistic, even enthusiastic, about it.

Let us not forget, in this connection, something of great importance. Whatever age may take away from you, it leaves you your imagination. You can still look and conjecture. What your body may not be able to do, your mind can.

For a woman, there is a distinct advantage in growing older. No longer need she worry about the side-effects of the Pill. According to the *Guinness Book of World Records*, "Medical literature contains extreme but unauthenticated cases of septuagenarian mothers." It goes on to say, however, that the oldest recorded mother of whom there is certain evidence is a woman who gave birth to a daughter on October 18, 1956, when her age was 57 years 129 days. Once menstruation is over, you can throw caution to the winds or wherever you want to throw it.

As for a man, it may buck up his ego to know that there is almost no limit to the age at which he may father a child. This same *Guinness Book of World Records* does not even attempt to cite a record in this category. It does, however, mention the case of the last Sharifian Emperor of Morocco, Moulay Ismail, known as "The Bloodthirsty," who is reputed to have fathered the most children: 548 sons and 340 daughters. What age he was when he fathered the 888th child I do not know. Nor do I know why he quit, unless from boredom.

Moulay Ismail, as you may have guessed, was polygamous. One wife would hardly have sufficed. Nonetheless the wife of Fyodor Vassilet of Russia produced the record number of 69 children, including 16 pairs of twins, 7 sets of triplets, and 4 sets of quadruplets, which isn't bad. Thirteen such women could have given Moulay his 888 children, in fact multiplying (and multiplying seems the appropriate word here) 13 times 69 the total is 897, a slight increase.

You who are having trouble remembering the names of your grandchildren and great-grandchildren, give a thought to Moulay Ismail. He may have had trouble remembering the names of all of his wives, not to mention his offspring.

Robert Browning, who lived to be seventy-seven and thus had at least a little experience with old age, is remembered for having said "Grow old along with me." I have always thought it generous of him to offer companionship, since it is nice to have someone to grow old with. But since Browning died in 1889, you who are growing old today will have to find someone else. So join me, if you would like. I may not carry you off to Italy, as Robert Browning carried off Elizabeth Barrett, but we can have a good time together right here, watching travel films.

2.

How Old Is Old?

Let me start this chapter with a piece of verse, "Age-Old Problem":

Of late I appear
To have reached that stage
When people look old
Who are only my age.

I do not remember when someone first called me old. This indicates either that my memory is failing or that it was a long time ago—or both. The only thing I am sure of is that the person who called me old was younger than I, probably quite a bit younger, someone I referred to as "a mere child," though perhaps with children of his or her own.

What I do remember is that I discovered my first gray hair when I was twenty, and promptly plucked it out. Two more gray hairs replaced the plucked one in a matter of days. I plucked the gray hairs for about two years, before giving up. Now, almost completely bald, I wish I had all those hairs back (and front). I cherish every hair, whatever its color.

Just as I was prematurely bald, I was probably prematurely old. I was "old before my time," as some people say. And that brings up the whole question of what "old" or "old age" is. Though I am no good at even the simplest arithmetic, I have been doing a little figuring, and I give you the results to mull over.

If there is a life expectancy of seventy-two years, a life expectancy that many of my friends are already beyond, it should be a simple matter to determine when old age begins. All you have to do is divide the seventy-two years into three parts: youth, middle age, and old age. That would mean that youth is the first twenty-four years, middle age the next twenty-four years, and old age the last twenty-four years. Or, to put it another way, middle age begins at twenty-five and old age begins at forty-nine.

I do not recommend, though, that you refer to any twenty-five-year-old of your acquaintance as middle aged, or that you call a forty-nine-year-old a senior citizen.

"How are you, old man?" I have found to be intended as a cordial, friendly greeting, without connotations of age. "Old man" in this context is warm and endearing, usually accompanied by a slap on the back. If you are really old, you may be knocked to the ground by this hearty salutation. But if you are merely what I think of as old (that is, only a little older than I am), you might stagger slightly but not go down.

In fact I have learned a few tricks about what to do if greeted too heartily. One is to fall into the back-slapper's arms in a gesture of extreme friendliness, thus avoiding a nasty bruise or even a fracture. Another, which is especially effective when younger or more athletic friends shake my hand with a viselike grip, is to go limp. This may be an admission of weakness, but it also spares me considerable pain.

"You are only as old as you feel," some people say. The trouble with this is that I feel older some days than others, or even from hour to hour. Since age is supposed to be progressive, it is confusing when you feel younger today than you did yesterday. If this kept up enough days and months and years, you could wind up in the cradle, chewing on a teething ring. But fortunately (or at least so I think, because I don't want to go through teething again), I have as many days I feel old as days I feel young, in fact a few more.

"You are only as old as you look" is another way of putting it. But there is so much trickery nowadays, with hairpieces and face lifting and all the rest, that it is increasingly hard to know how old anyone is by the way he or she looks. The only time you get much of an idea is when you look at yourself in a mirror, under a strong light, after removing such hair, teeth, and other parts as were not given to you by Nature. I may be dodging the issue, but when I am stripped down this way, I simply don't look in the mirror. In fact I look at my reflection less and less every year, though I reflect more than ever.

No, age is merely a comparative matter. You are older than some and younger than some. In a way, being around young people keeps me young, at least in attitude, but at the same time it makes me feel old to know that they are younger than I and that they think me old, sometimes older than I really am. On the other hand, being around old people (i.e., people older than I) makes me seem young, at least chronologically. But I am afraid that being around them will cause me to be considered one of the group, another old oldster.

This is especially poignant for me, because I live in a college town which is also a favorite place for retirement homes. I see young people a great deal, but I see old people a great deal too. Several times in one day I may move from one circle to another, being now the oldest among young people and then the youngest among old people.

It's a little like going from hot water to cold water, back and forth. But like a Finn leaving a hot sauna for a romp in the snow, I find it invigorating. Of course there is always the chance of psychological pneumonia. However, I get a thrill out of living dangerously, just as I do out of living at all.

Much as I enjoy being around young people and being accepted by them (I think), not as one of them but as an acceptable old fellow, I am probably happier being among those who are older than I am.

"Old So-and-So is fifteen years older than I, and still going strong," I often say. Of course old So-and-So may not be going as strong as I think, just as I am not going as strong as he thinks anyone fifteen years younger must be going. I remember a recent conversation with him.

"I can't believe you're as old as you are," I said. Then I quickly added, lest this be misconstrued, "You could pass for ten years younger."

"Thanks," he said. "I feel pretty good. Walked five miles today."

He knows I walk only two miles, and then only on Mondays, Wednesdays, and Fridays, provided the weather is good. That "five miles" of his was definitely a put-down. I realized, too late, that he was a little annoyed at my saying he could pass for ten years younger, when he thought he could pass for twenty years younger.

There was an awkward pause while I waited for him to say I could pass for ten years younger myself, or even five.

He didn't, though. And I suddenly felt as old as I am.

Flattery, they say, will get you nowhere, but I don't believe it. Tell someone he or she looks ten, twenty, or thirty years younger than the age you know the person to be and you will get yourself a very happy companion.

This applies, however, only to old people. Young people want to be thought older than they are. Try telling someone who says he is thirty, "I don't believe it. You look ten years younger than that!"

One answer, therefore, to the question "How old is old?" is that old is when you want to be told you look younger than you are.

There is one time when people not only wish to be told they seem older than the age they tell you they are but actually *tell* you they are older than they are. This is when they are *very* old and want to be thought still older out of sheer pride in longevity.

I have already referred to the *Guinness Book of World Records*. Let me refer to it again on this matter of very old age. "No single subject is more obscured by vanity, deceit, falsehood, and deliberate fraud," say the editors of this compilation of records, "than the extremes of human longevity." Then, becoming slightly irate, they go on: "Many hundreds of claims throughout history have been made for persons living well into their second century and some, insulting to the intelligence, for people living even into their third."

They are more than a little dubious about the news item from Peking stating that Li Chung-yun, the "oldest man on earth," had just died at the age of 256 years. Nor do they give much credence to the claim of 164 years for Shirali Muslimov of

Azerbaijan, U.S.S.R. Brushing past Larak, a god-King who according to Sumerian mythology lived 28,800 years, and our old friend (really old) Methuselah, they say: "The greatest authenticated age to which a human has ever lived is 113 years 124 days in the case of Pierre Joubert, a French-Canadian bootmaker." How the man lived so long in a bootmaker's case, they do not explain.

You know, of course, of the fictional Shangri-la, where everyone lived on and on in the most idyllic and genteel fashion. Apparently nonfictional are recent discoveries by anthropologists who have conducted studies in remote parts of the world. These scientists have come upon primitive tribes which enjoy extreme longevity, thanks to a high-protein diet of raw meat and the regular exercise obtained by running (1) after animals that would provide such meat and (2) away from animals for which they themselves would provide the same.

Theirs may be a long life, but without electricity or even a knife and fork, not one I would choose. It reminds me of an item I happened upon in a medical journal: "When three tribesmen from an isolated tribe were discovered recently in the Philippine rain forests, the dentists who examined their mouths found that though their teeth were filed and blackened, not one of the men had a single cavity." Just as you might live longer in a primitive society, subsisting on raw meat and without the comforts you have come to take for granted, apparently you can be free of cavities if you are willing to join a tribe in the Philippine rain forest and have teeth as black as theirs.

However, there is no question that people are living longer, in highly civilized parts of the world, even as they live better. This raises an interesting point that I have tried to summarize in the following lines, entitled "Good Maker":

They really don't make things as well today.
Take cars—they don't last half as long, I say—
And faucets dribble and gaskets slip.
Today there's no pride in workmanship.
But be of good cheer and rejoice with me
At ever increasing longevity.
Yes, Someone has pride and Someone is clever,
For *people* are lasting longer than ever.

The fact remains that while some people are a little apologetic about being somewhat old, they take pride in being very old. My great-grandfather (actually my step-great-grandfather) lived to be ninety-nine. As a small boy I can remember his proudly saying "I'm going on a hundred" or "I'm in my hundredth year."

But except for the very old, most old people want to be considered younger than they really are. It is not always a matter of being told they look younger. Sometimes, in truth, this is impossible on the face of it, and I do mean on the face of it.

I know a woman who is eighty-six and looks eighty-six. I cannot force myself to say to her, "You could pass for seventy." She wouldn't believe it if

I told her. She might even be offended, thinking I was making fun of her, or more likely that I was buttering her up, perhaps hoping she would leave me something in her will.

What I tell her instead, in complete honesty, is something like "You have a wonderfully young outlook."

An outlook, you see, doesn't have to get gray or wrinkled or bent. Often it does, but it doesn't have to, and this woman of eighty-six has a beautiful outlook. She is pleased with her family, even her in-laws. She is more amused than amazed at the way young people act and the way they talk. She watches TV, but not all the time. She reads the newspaper and, better still, reads books, including some of mine. She will talk or she will listen. She doesn't think the world is going to the dogs (though she likes dogs and wouldn't deprive them of anything), but she is well aware of the fact that the world is going—that is, changing.

I hope I have a young outlook. Since I have an old everything else, this is my one chance at having a bit of youth as a part of me. I am not sure it is possible to acquire, or to hang onto, a young outlook, but I have a few suggestions, none of them involving surgery or medication.

One is to look for a moment at that word "outlook." It means looking out, instead of looking in. Maybe it is unnecessary to refer to a young outlook, since the habit of looking out instead of looking in is itself youthful—except in adolescents. One of the worst features of teenagers is looking in or, as they put it, "finding yourself." I don't consider looking out at a mirror, which teenagers can do for hours, real outlook. It is just the opposite. It is looking out in order to look in. What is usually seen is a slightly enlarged ego, or maybe an ill id.

And yet one way for anyone who is old to have a young outlook, or simply an outlook, is to be around young people as much as possible. By as much as possible I mean as much as they will let you. Young people naturally enough want to be with young people. To be old, but sensibly old, is to be with the young, whether your children and grandchildren or others', as much as you can but not to overdo it. Young people can stand old people (if I am a fair sample) only about so long. And vice versa.

How old is old? I really don't know. But I do know that there are different kinds of old, or of old age. One is chronological, merely adding up the years. This you cannot avoid. It is also what you may be able to keep a secret from your friends and acquaintances but will have to put down on your Social Security and Medicare applications and (if you can still get one) on your driver's license.

Another kind of old age is physical. Not being an M.D., I can't help you much in this regard, though I shall have something to say about it in a subsequent chapter.

Still another kind, and one of the most important, is mental or psychological age, involving the "outlook" I have already described.

With longevity increasing, old age is coming later and lasting longer. What was old age only a generation or so ago is now middle age. It is getting harder and harder to say, categorically, how old one has to be to be old.

I like fun, and I think a challenge is fun, and I know old age is a challenge. Therefore old age is, or can be, fun. Making people think, without too obviously trying, that I am younger than my chronological age is becoming more of a challenge, and therefore more fun, every year.

But like my step-great-grandfather, when I'm ninety-nine I hope I'll be ready both to boost and to boast about my age. I can hardly wait to say, the day after my ninety-ninth birthday (and I hope I have the lungpower to blow out ninety-nine candles), "I'm going on a hundred."

3.

Looking Forward To and Sideways At Retirement

"**R**etirement" and "retiring" are odd words. They could have to do with putting a new tire on a car. Or being tired once and getting tired all over again. Or, as stated in a couplet and with a slightly different twist:

> Retired is being tired twice, I've thought:
> First tired of working, then tired of not.

When I was a small child, in fact most of my early life, I was considered and sometimes called right to my face "shy and retiring." The shy part was correct. I was often shy such things as money and confidence. But the retiring part was silly. Not only was I unable to afford it, but my parents wouldn't have let me. I still had to get through school and find a job and get married and do a lot of other things.

Those of course were the Old Days. (Days, you

see, can be old too, just like people.) Youngsters today sometimes retire in their teens, only it is called dropping out. The difference between this and real retirement is that the dropout can, after a few years, drop in again. Anyone who retires because of age is more likely to stay retired, either from choice or from necessity.

However, as I shall discuss shortly, it is possible to retire and then embark upon a new career, as is being done increasingly. This can lead to a second retirement and even a third.

"I am retiring" once had still another meaning. It meant "I am going to bed." It likewise usually meant that you were going to your own bed. Now people just say forthrightly, "I'm going to bed," and it's none of your business with whom.

Most people retire when they are sixty or sixty-five, and what I am considering now has little to do with going to bed, except that after you have retired, in the through-working sense, you can stay in bed longer in the morning if you wish. When my young neighbor drives out of his driveway next to my bedroom at 7:30 A.M., he invariably wakes me up. But I turn over and go back to sleep, with a satisfied sigh and a faint smile on my lips.

The poor fellow. He is only forty-five, and has another twenty years of getting up early, gulping down his breakfast, and hoping his car will start so he can get to work by eight. He also has another twenty years of worrying, in his business, about supplies, sales, competition, strikes, and whether he himself will be laid off or, a euphemism for the same thing, forced into "early retirement."

I have said that I was prematurely gray and prematurely old. I also retired prematurely. But I hasten to say that it was not early retirement in the above sense. It was not forced on me. I retired, of my own choice, nine years before I had to.

What I did, however, was not really to retire but to make my avocation my vocation. This might be considered, by an honest-to-goodness retirer, to be cheating. But it is one way of easing out, though since I work harder since my so-called retirement than before, "easing" doesn't seem quite the word for it. The main difference is that I am now my own master and set my own working hours.

Nevertheless, more and more people are taking optional early retirement, getting out while the getting is good, or while there is still some chance of getting. It has its disadvantages. Giving up a regular job to take an irregular one is risky. Speaking for myself, I am sometimes uncertain, when faced with a questionnaire, whether I should put down "Self-employed" or "Unemployed." The terms can be disconcertingly synonymous.

There is also the chance that you will be called "retired" before you want to be. Being retired, at however early an age, may make you seem older than you are, which of course you wish to avoid at all costs. Moreover, the word that you have retired gets around with remarkable speed, and very soon there are requests for your time and your money, especially your money. The assumption is that anyone who retires early must be loaded, and people quickly gather around to help unload you.

But there are important advantages to retiring early, if you have something else you can do and would prefer to do, or if you want to start doing nothing sooner than most are able to. There is also a kind of middle-of-the-road alternative, not quite the same as either doing something different or doing nothing. That is, to retire in order to be under less pressure and to do less than you had been doing and therefore perhaps be able to do it longer.

I come of a short-lived family. As I write this, I have lived eight years longer than any male in my family for three generations. It is true that there have not been many males in my family, and that the shortest-lived, my grandfather, who lived to be only forty-nine, picked a pimple on his lip and died of blood poisoning. I have had more pimples on my lip and elsewhere than my grandfather, but with his early demise in mind I have picked them with care and doused them with a powerful antiseptic.

My grandfather was a pharmacist, back in the mortar-and-pestle days, and I have never been able to understand his failure to take the proper precautions.

Anyhow, the possibility of my not living to what is called a ripe old age was one reason for my early retirement, or my early escape from what I once described in the following lines:

As I often remark when I'm low as can be,
　It's a terrible rat race I'm in,
And what is still worse, I'm beginning to see,
　The rats are quite likely to win.

I didn't desert a sinking ship, as rats are supposed to do. The ship is still afloat. I must confess I am a little annoyed that it continues to sail so well without me.

Discovering that you are not indispensable can be one of the harshest blows of retirement.

Doctors, lawyers, and those who own their own businesses can postpone retirement indefinitely, and sometimes do so a little too long. I have a dentist who will probably go on working as long as he is able to pick at a spot of decay. I hate to think of choosing (I started to say picking) another dentist, so I hope his eyes hold out as long as my teeth do.

There are those, as I have intimated, who retire several times. They retire early, go into something else for a few years, retire from that, go into still another enterprise, perhaps part-time, retire from that, and so on. I have a friend who has retired five times, almost equaling the farewell performances of Sarah Bernhardt, who by the way lived to be seventy-eight and went on acting after she met with an accident and had to have one leg amputated. She had an artificial leg, however, which saved her from disconcertingly hopping around the stage while playing the leading role in *Camille*.

The Divine Sarah is an inspiration to those in their late seventies with two perfectly good legs who are thinking of going back to work.

The best thing about repeated retirement, according to my friend who has retired five times, is all the retirement parties and the loot that goes with them. He has two gold watches and an entire wall covered with plaques. In his den the mantel sags a little under the weight of silver cups and bowls as well as medallions in plush-back frames. He also has a row of scrapbooks in his bookcase, each filled with photos and testimonials.

"It's a little like having had five wives," he tells me. Since I have had only one wife, I am not exactly sure of what he means. But apparently there is something good about it. Perhaps variety is the spice of wife.

William Cowper, who died in 1800 at the age of sixty-nine, wrote a poem called *Retirement*. In it he remarks:

> Absence of occupation is not rest,
> A mind quite vacant is a mind distress'd.

That may be why my friend kept coming out of retirement. He was afraid that if he were not occupied his mind would go vacant. It is what worries many people about retirement. They are worried almost as much as the owner of a motel who has a neon-lighted "Vacancy" sign out in front of his place night after night. He has a mind distressed, sure enough, but since he owns the motel he is spared the prospect of having to retire at sixty-five. Bankruptcy, perhaps, but not retirement.

Despite the example I have given, most people retire only once. Unless retirement is caused by ill health, they know precisely when they are going to retire—at sixty or sixty-five or whatever age the institution they work for requires. Thus retirement is more definite than life expectancy, which is something that everyone (but me, with my poor genes) expects to go beyond. If a definite retirement age is in the rules, you can figure out exactly how long you have before you get to it, whether you like it or not.

This brings up an interesting difference in people. I have known those who dreaded retirement, and I have known those who could hardly wait. If you can manage it, you should try to get into the latter category.

I have a friend who looked forward to retirement more than anyone else I have ever known. It was not that he was in such difficult or unpleasant work. Well, maybe he was. He was the Dean of the Faculty at a college. The more I think about it, the more I think it was his line of work that made him so impatient to retire. Had he been in something less involved with human relationships, such as bricklaying, or in a profession in which his authority would have been less in question, like that of a high-ranking Army officer, he might not have kept that calendar on his desk, checking off the years and months.

I know how he felt, because my first retirement was also from the job of Dean of the Faculty. Not the same faculty, but then aren't all faculties much alike?

As I have said, I retired early, nine years early, while he stuck it out, building up his retirement income even as he dreamed of those wonderful years of freedom ahead. Academic freedom, to him, meant freedom from academic chores and academic people, such as ultra-conservative trustees, ultra-liberal professors, and ultra-demanding students.

Since I retired so long before he did, although we are within a few months of the same age, his envy was ill disguised.

"Must be great, being retired," was the way he opened most of our conversations.

"But I didn't really retire. I just quit in order to go into something else," I always insisted.

"Nevertheless you retired," he said stubbornly.

Then I waited expectantly. I knew what was coming, and it always came.

"Just three more years and five months," he said, with a wistful, dreamy look in his eyes.

There are some, I know, who look forward

eagerly to retirement and then hate it after the first week. But this man, I am happy to report, loved retirement from the beginning and still loves it.

His is not an absence of occupation or a vacant mind. He has a Project. Whether he ever finishes the Project is of no great importance. It gives him something to think about, something to talk about, something to justify a certain amount of travel. Furthermore it is a Large Project. It is something that should keep him busy, or as busy as he wants to keep himself, for many years.

Unlike his looking forward to retirement and counting the days, I think he takes the opposite view of his Project. He would not like to see it concluded too soon, because then it would be not as if he had retired but his Project had. He would be hard pressed to find another Project as long-range, significant, and satisfying.

Anyhow, he is the example I usually cite when I am asked (which is not very often) to tell about someone who could hardly wait to retire and then found retirement as wonderful as he had anticipated. I like to see people happy, and he is a happy man.

But you do not need a Project. A Hobby serves much the same purpose, though I think a Project is superior, or at least the person who has one thinks so. A Hobby is something you became interested in long before retirement and gave your spare time to and perhaps became skilled at. It is defined as "a favorite avocation." But I think of a Hobby as something you dabble in, fool around with. A Project, by contrast, is something you *plan* to do, something projected into the future—i.e., after retirement, when you at last have the time for it. It may also be something of greater importance in its consequences for you and for the human race (if you manage to accomplish it) than a Hobby.

I do not mean to denigrate hobbies. They are fine, both before and after retirement. But observation of this friend of mine, so idyllically happy in retirement, makes me aware of the special significance of a Project.

My friend is taking his time with his Project, and wisely. After all, it is his own Project and it is his own time.

Time, you see, is what retirement is all about. You may not know precisely how much you have of it, but it is all yours, to do with as you wish. In fact you yourself are yours. You are your own man, or woman. Unless you have a bossy spouse, or like to boss yourself around, you have no boss. If you want it that way, every day can be one big coffee break. If you don't want it that way, you can work as much or as little as you want to on your Project, your Hobby, or whatever. And, curiously, the work won't seem like work.

Retirement is when there is time to think, and you must be careful not to stop thinking just because you *think* you have "all the time in the world" and can put off thinking, like everything else, until tomorrow.

There are books you can read that will make you think, and there are books (and TV programs) that will give you a respite from thinking, especially from thinking about yourself.

The retired people I have found the most happy with retirement are those who are "on the go." And you can be on the go mentally as well as (or better than) physically. You can be on the go in a wheelchair, without turning a wheel—if the wheels are turning in your head.

I have discovered that people who were dull and dissatisfied before retirement are also dull and dissatisfied after retirement, and keep getting more so.

On the brighter side, I know a woman in her eighties who is the liveliest person at any party. She reads, she studies (maybe starting another foreign language, to add to the four or five she already knows), she travels to distant, exotic places. She visits her far-flung children and grandchildren and great-grandchildren. The remarkable thing is that they clamor for her to visit them, and really mean it. How does she know they mean it? They send her the plane fare.

What her Project is, or maybe in this instance it's a Hobby, is *life*. People interest her, and she interests people. She gives herself, including both her time and her money, to those who are in need.

I have taken her as my model, or one of my models. And I have learned from her that you can retire from a job but you can't, or shouldn't, retire from life.

4.

And Now Where Shall We Live?

The title of this chapter brings to mind some lines at the end of Milton's *Paradise Lost*. Adam and Eve, having sinned by eating the forbidden fruit, are banished from Eden. As they look back, they drop a few tears, but wipe them soon:

The world was all before them, where to choose
Their place of rest, and Providence their guide.

The retiree may not have sinned, or not in such an original way as Adam and Eve, may not have been banished from a longtime and congenial place of residence, may not drop even a single tear. But Milton's lines have significance for everyone who has retired and is now thinking of moving to a smaller dwelling, a better climate, nearer the children, or whatever. Even for those who do not move, retirement is a moving experience.

Adam and Eve had an advantage over most of us—being able to choose any place in the world, and the world not then being full of people, air pollution, and high-priced real estate. How Adam and Eve were going to get around to look things over, Milton does not say, but they had a helpful guide, named Providence. They could live anywhere they wished, except for Eden, and while they were still much too young for Social Security, finances seemed to be no problem.

But we have an advantage over Adam and Eve. We can stay in Eden, if we wish to. We don't have to move. Or we can find a town named Eden in Georgia, Idaho, Illinois, Maryland, Michigan, New York, South Dakota, Texas, Vermont, Wisconsin, and Wyoming, as well as an Edon in Ohio and an Eden Isle in Arkansas. Whether all of these Edens are paradises, as was the original, I am not sure, since I have never had the pleasure of visiting any of them. I have, however, written a poem about Eden that if not quite so poetic is at least somewhat shorter than *Paradise Lost* or, indeed, anything Milton ever wrote. My poem, not as yet required in any English course, is:

There wasn't a weed in
The Garden of Eden.

Enough of this. I have been led astray by Eden, just as Adam and Eve were. The Serpent is still at work, and it just happens that I ate an apple before beginning this chapter. Before returning to the subject of retirement, however, let me remind you that although Milton left Adam and Eve evicted from their idyllic home at the end of *Paradise Lost,* he relented and wrote *Paradise Regained.*

Anyhow, most people have thoughts of moving when they retire. Now that they are free, they may consider moving to a more Edenlike community, one where there is less rain or more rain, where there is less smog (never where there is more smog), where it is warmer in the winter, and where they are closer to such important facilities as a shopping center, an art museum, a library, or, to be more practical and honest, a hospital.

They may think not so much of moving *to* something as *away from* something. In the latter case it may be a large, weed-infested lawn or a neighbor's barking dog or the demands of numerous social and do-good enterprises. If you are like me and lack the nerve to resign, this may be the only way to get out of a certain club or off a time-consuming committee. Here, at last, is a chance to chuck it all.

"Sorry," you can say, "but we are moving to ——." Just be sure, if this is your motivation, that you are moving far enough away that there is no question about your driving back for meetings or fund-raising events. That could make matters worse instead of better. I would say a hundred miles is the minimum. A thousand miles is safer.

The decision of whether and where to move is so difficult that many people put it off, and at the same time celebrate their gaining the freedom of retirement by going on a trip. Ideally, one should take a round-the-world cruise and stay away for six months or even, settling for a while in some such place as Japan or England, a full year.

You say this is too expensive? Nonsense. If you put one dollar a day into a king-size piggy bank or under your mattress for thirty years you will have a travel fund of $10,950 or, if a man and wife both do this, a fund of $21,900. If you put the money under your mattress, in dollar bills, you may wish to exchange them for bills of larger denomination now and then, or your bed may seem a little lumpy after about twenty-five years. I have not figured out how much you would have if you placed the money in a savings account, but it would be considerably more than $21,900 for two persons by the time of retirement, even allowing for the cost of gasoline and tires, going to the bank or savings and loan every day.

On that amount of money, saved almost without noticing it, you could take a long retirement cruise or stay the whole year in Paris, on the Right Bank at that, if you didn't do too much shopping. You would be as free as a bird. Or, to put it another way, have quite a lark. Best of all you would be ready to come home. In fact during the last three or four months you would be eager to come home.

But when you got home, after you had told everyone (several times) about your "fabulous trip," you would start thinking again about whether you should move and if so where. You would get plenty of advice about where, each of your friends having a favorite spot.

"You'll love it there," they will say, with a wistful, dreamy look in their eyes.

But could it be that they are not your friends after all? Do they simply want you to move away —anywhere? If they have themselves retired but haven't moved to the place they suggest, though they have had both the freedom and the means to do so, I would be suspicious.

"Why haven't you moved there yourselves?" you might ask. That's what I do, and then I listen carefully to each word and watch every facial expression and wish I owned a lie detector. I have come to some interesting conclusions.

Though I am, as I have said, between my first and second retirements, we could move. There is no impediment. We have talked about it many times and have even, in our familiar phrase, been "on the verge." But the verge is as far as we ever get, and I know why. We have seen prettier places, more exciting places, places where the air is better, but the years go by and we stay where we are because of:

1. Friends, including those who instead of urging us to go elsewhere beg us to stay here.

2. Familiarity, which involves knowing where things are and how to get to them, as well as the best shop for clothes, the best supermarket for groceries, and the best restaurants for good food

and service at reasonable prices. (When I say reasonable I mean low.)

3. Indecision, inertia. Whatever you call it, this is probably the most important. Put simply, not moving is easier than moving, and the older I get the more I like what is easy.

That third reason is also why we have not as yet made another kind of move—not from one town to another but from a house to an apartment. We have friends who, as soon as they retired, or as soon as they could find a buyer, sold their home. Now they live in an apartment, and sometimes they drive me wild with envy.

"No yard to take care of," the husband says, watching me as I try surreptitiously to remove a bit of dirt from under a fingernail.

"When you want to go away for a week or a month," says the wife, "you just lock the door and walk out."

"Great security, too," puts in the husband. "Burglar alarm system, nightwatchman, all the rest."

"Fire sprinklers in the ceiling of every room," adds the wife.

They don't have to tell me about the view. They are on the twelfth floor of a condominium and look out across the city, all the way to the ocean. The lights at night are terrific. By contrast, we in our one-story tract house look across the street at another one-story tract house.

Then why don't we move to an apartment? Our retired friends tell us there is an apartment for sale in their condominium, with an even better view than theirs, and they think we could get a good deal on it because the owner is being transferred by his company and has to move quickly.

I mentioned inertia. If there is such a thing as the opposite, or ertia, it would take a bundle of it for us to move out of our house. We could never get all of our belongings into an apartment, and we would not give up a stick of furniture. It is with these sticks that we are stuck, besides the books and bric-a-brac on the shelves, the pictures on the walls, and the carpets on the floors.

Our house is full of heirlooms, handed down by our parents and grandparents and great-grandparents, some of them Sears, Roebuck originals. There are also the items of sentimental value that we have brought back from our travels, such as the monkeypod back scratcher we bought in Honolulu and the Colonial jug, in the likeness of Benjamin Franklin, that we picked up at a sale in Boston.

No apartment would have as many closets as our house, and our closets are full, despite the lavish tax-deductible gifts we make each year to the Salvation Army, Good Will, and Disabled War Veterans. Each time we start getting serious about moving to an apartment, all we have to do is open a closet door, and we decide to stay put, at least for a few more years.

"I couldn't face it," my wife says. What she means is that she couldn't face moving once she has faced the contents of even one closet.

"I couldn't either," I say, glad once again to find us in such satisfying agreement.

All of this is aside from the problem of which child should get what, if we should try to keep things in the family instead of giving them to some worthy cause. Should we designate certain items for each child? Should we base it on age, the eldest having his pick, or on need? Should we let them have alternate choices, after drawing lots to see who would start first?

And what if they should say, as we looked on anxiously, "It's all old-fashioned stuff. We don't want any of it." Do you blame us if we avoid, or postpone, the issue?

Aside from the above-mentioned difficulties of moving from a house to an apartment, there is real doubt about how we would get along without a lawn to mow or a garden to tend. It is not the closeness to nature I have in mind, not the pride in the flower that came into being because we planted the seed and watered and cultivated and sprayed and pruned. What I am thinking of is the exercise, ideal for us old folks who have been told we had better not overdo the situps and the jogging, even the running in place.

For those who are up to it, pushing a lawn mower is excellent for the lungs, the legs, the triceps and pectorals. You can stop and rest whenever you want to, perhaps needing to empty the catcher anyhow. For those for whom this is too demanding, growing roses or camellias gets you out in the open and provides a modicum of exercise with the bending over and straightening up, along with a little hoeing and now and then squeezing a pair of clippers.

You can always pause to admire your handiwork, or you can send the blood coursing through your arteries by fighting off a bee. When you have completed your gardening task you will not only have worked up an appetite, or justified a nap, but have accomplished a little something by way of helping Mother Nature, who is even older than you are.

Ecology is not just for the young, though they may think they are the ones who invented it.

Yes, living in an apartment, especially in a modern high-rise condominium, has its advantages. But there are also advantages in living as long as you can in your own house and keeping in touch with the good earth.

I almost forgot to say that you may happen to like your house, even love it, as we do ours. To paraphrase the song from *My Fair Lady*, "I've grown accustomed to the place." Giving it up would be like giving up a member of the family.

An even greater decision than whether to move from one's house to an apartment is whether to skip the move to the apartment and move to a retirement home. My wife and I argue almost daily over this.

"Let's go—when we go—directly to a retirement home," she says, "and save having to move twice."

"I'd rather take it gradually," I say. "First an

apartment and then a retirement home. One step at a time."

"There's a waiting list. If we apply now we'll still have to wait three or four years to get into the Green Acre Gardens," she says.

"And meanwhile have all that down payment tied up," I say. (It occurs to me, for the first time, that I have never heard of an up payment tied down, but that is neither here nor there, especially not here.)

I have visited a number of retirement homes, some of them much better than others. Many have little cottages that give you the illusion of never having left home, with gardens you can either tend or leave to the management. One retirement home was like a huge resort hotel, or like a cruise ship. Residents took their morning "constitutional" by walking around the top. Seven times around was one mile, they told me, when I could walk briskly enough to keep up with them. If you got out of breath, you could stop and pretend to be admiring the view, or imagine you were a seasick passenger leaning over the rail.

The food in retirement homes varies from the institutional-subsistence level to the very good indeed. By very good indeed I mean better than what we get at home and as good as in most restaurants.

Food becomes more and more important, in fact more and more of a game, as you grow older. It is not that you eat more. You probably eat less. But you may have to avoid certain things not permitted in your diet. You may have to ask for a sugar substitute. You may have to cut down on the salt that in your younger days you sprinkled freely over everything—before tasting. The instructions on your bottle of pills for whatever ails you, and something probably does, instructs you to "Take three times a day with meals." Indeed, taking pills may be the reason you eat three times a day instead of two or four.

I say this with considerable assurance and authority, because it all applies to me, including the pills, which in my case (and I am quite a case) are for high blood pressure, medium arthritis, and low spirits.

I am referring now only to the pills I take with my meals. There are others I take when I get up, which I do with difficulty, and still others I take when I go to bed, just before I say my prayers, which include a request that the pills do their prescribed work.

But the main reason most elderly people are so preoccupied with eating is that it is something to do. At retirement homes, as I have observed, most residents want to be in the first sitting, and the rush to the tables for lunch and dinner is like the scramble to get onto a crowded bus or out of a burning building. As a visitor, I have twice been very nearly knocked down and run over. It reminded me of the running of the bulls at Pamplona.

The seating in retirement homes fascinates me and again tests my weak and ever-weakening

45

powers of decision. Would I select a retirement home with the freedom to sit anywhere you wish, but with the lack of a sense of belonging and of constant companionship? Or would I choose a retirement home where you are assigned a table and have to stay there the rest of your days, with the advantage of developing a familial relationship with those at your regular table but the risk of being stuck with someone you cannot stand? Or would I seek out one of those retirement homes where, I am told, they assign you to a table, but for only three months?

Frankly, I don't know which would be better. I like the freedom and variety of the first method, but I also like the nesting quality of the second and third. It is the regular-table procedure that causes me to recall a news item I saw not long ago: "Though it may seem archaic, the napkin ring is making a comeback." It led me to write these nostalgic lines, which I called "Give Me a Ring":

> Consider that forgotten thing,
> Once popular, the napkin ring.
> When you had eaten, like a clown
> You didn't throw your napkin down
> But rolled it up and stuffed it through
> A ring. It was the thing to do.
>
> It saved on laundry, wear and tear.
> That's why that ring was always there,
> A ring that bore your name, right by you,

Or something to identify you.
The napkin of another chap
Must never reach your mouth—or lap.

What pride you had in ownership
Each time you wiped your chin or lip.
How good you felt to know you saved
On laundry bills or those who slaved.
But best, your ring upon the rack,
To know you were expected back.

Yes, if you always sat at the same table at a retirement home you would be expected back, and if you didn't show up they would send someone out looking for you. This might give you a homey, wanted feeling. But then again you might be trying to escape.

I know I shall probably wind up, or wind down, in a retirement home—or my wife will, without me. I would probably adjust to it, even come to love it as many of my friends have. It is the easiest, safest life of all. I would be with my chronological, if not always ideological, fellows. Medical care would be close at hand, perhaps as close as a warning button by my bed and another in the bathroom.

But I am putting it off, while I consider the intermediate move to an apartment. By the time I make up my mind, which is harder to make up than my bed, and changed more often, I may be too old to get in.

Meanwhile time flies, which is something *I* have

never been able to do. But I could dress up like Batman and go down to the local retirement home and give them a thrill. Since they always like a little entertainment, they might jump me over a hundred others and put me at the top of the waiting list.

5.

Taking Advantage of the Advantages

Now that I have decided for everyone else, but not for myself, where to live after retirement, I must get into a topic that it has been hard for me to put off this long. It is something that I think has been overlooked by many, and it is easy to see why.

I want to discuss the advantages of growing old.

For one thing, it is a great satisfaction to be around fewer and fewer people who can say "You are too young to remember. . . ." Or "That was before your time." Or "When I was your age. . . ." I myself now know the pleasure of saying such things, effectively putting down the young, including those who are only in their early sixties.

The other night I was at a dinner party, holding everyone spellbound with comments on what was ancient history to some and medieval history to others but personal history to me.

First, of course, I looked around to make sure

that no one was as old as I. Increasingly I find it unnecessary to make any such preliminary survey of my companions. Then I steered the subject over to the American presidents.

"I didn't know Theodore Roosevelt personally," I said, "but I have a vivid recollection of him as President." I did not add that my mind was especially active when I was two years old, going on three, at the time the first Roosevelt concluded his term of office.

Then I brought up my prize story, about the first President I actually shook hands with. I wish I could say it was Lincoln, or even Woodrow Wilson, who was President when I was in high school and might indeed have been the one I shook hands with if I had gone to a different high school, one closer to Washington, D.C. But I was honest about it.

"The first President I shook hands with was Warren G. Harding," I said, and then went into great detail about how it happened and how handsome Harding looked in his white Palm Beach suit. I neglected to mention that Harding is generally considered the poorest of our Presidents. But I got extra points, as a piece of living history, by saying "The *first* President I shook hands with," because this left the impression, without my actually saying so, that I shook hands with a great many others, from Coolidge and Hoover to the present.

If, at some other gathering, the talk should turn

to war, I can always give my personal impressions not of the Spanish-American War, which I barely missed, but of World War I. True, I did not serve in the trenches Over There and was not under fire at the Battle of Belleau Wood, but I was old enough to read about the war day after day in the newspapers, starting back in 1914. I was in junior high school ROTC, carrying a wooden gun, when the Armistice was signed (much to my relief, because I admit to being a coward) in 1918.

I try to hide the sneer on my face when some young whippersnapper pipes up with something he learned about World War I from a history textbook.

"It was different, living through it," I say. "You wouldn't understand."

In the Army (and Navy and Air Force and Marines) there is what is called "pulling your rank." What I am suggesting is that there is also something that I would call "pulling your age." Over sixty is like being a major. Over seventy is like being a colonel. Over eighty is like being a brigadier or major general. Over ninety is like being a four-star general. Over a hundred is like being a five-star absolutely full General. As you know, there aren't many with that exalted rank, and their every utterance is news.

Anyone reaching a hundred is sure to get an interview and his picture in the paper.

"To what do you attribute your success in reaching the century mark?" asks the reporter.

"Keeping away from cigarettes and liquor and women," says one centenarian.

"Smoking *see*gars and drinking rotgut whiskey," says another, who merely winks and leers at the mention of women.

"Staying alive a hundred years," says still another, who has no fancy ideas about longevity.

If I live to be a hundred, I don't know what I'll say. When I get around ninety-five I'll start thinking up statements to give to the press. I know I'll be something of a show-off, and I may do a few pushups, especially if I'm on TV.

I can tell you this. I'll be proud. I'll make the most of it. As it is, I am envious of people who are ninety. They may not have lived it up, but they have lived. They have survived wars and depressions and taxes and viruses and muggers and drunken drivers. More than that, the world has survived too, despite dire predictions to the contrary.

But even if I don't make it to a hundred, I have already experienced some of the advantages and satisfactions of growing old. I have previously mentioned being able to outage people, which is a little like upstaging them. Let me tell you about something else I enjoy immensely.

At dinner parties, my wife and I are often the oldest persons present. We therefore consider it our privilege, and our friends concede it, to be the first to leave.

We used to stay on and on at a party, until eleven o'clock or later, while the small talk got smaller and smaller and everyone got sleepier and sleepier (or at least we did) but no one had the nerve to leave. It's different now.

About nine-fifty I look at my watch and then stand up, full of the authority of age.

"It's time for us old folks to go," I say. "We have to get our rest."

There is complete understanding. No one objects. Of course it may be that the young folks are glad to be rid of us so that they can talk about things they think we wouldn't understand or that might shock us. But I like to believe that they respect us and think we have earned the right to leave a little early. There may be those who envy us and say to themselves, "If only we had a good excuse like that."

Or consider another advantage or privilege that comes with age. I have in mind the fact that, although I own a car and have a license to drive it (if I wear my glasses), our younger friends think driving too demanding and exhausting for a person of my age.

"We'll pick you up tonight," they say, and insist on it.

I must confess that I encourage this with occasional hints about my weakening vision and slowing reflexes. Our friends have become fearful of my being on the highway, thinking not only of me but of those whom I might endanger, such as innocent women and children. What I know for sure is that they are thinking of themselves, as I learn when I offer to do the driving.

"Oh, no! You must let us drive *you*," they say, with an ill-disguised look of fright. "It isn't out of the way at all. And we need to get some mileage on our new car."

They not only drive us wherever we are going but help us in and out of the car with tenderness and solicitude. My wife thinks it a little absurd, but I like it, especially when it is a two-door car and I sit in the back. Frankly, a little help is helpful.

Mostly I think of all that saving of gasoline and oil and tires. Our car is old (cars grow old, too) and I see no point in buying a new one, we have so few miles on it. I wish I had worn a pedometer all my life. Then I would know not only how old I am but what my mileage is.

Another advantage of growing old is forgetting. At first you may think this a disadvantage, but I assure you it isn't. Not, that is, if you do it right.

What I have in mind is selective forgetting. All you have to do is forget what you don't want to remember. I have become an expert at this. How else could the old days be the Good Old Days? There must have been some bad things, back when I was a boy and a young man, and even when I was middle-aged. But I, like many others, remember only what I want to remember and forget all the rest. Actually, I suppose, the old days were the Good-and-Bad Old Days.

Sometimes I remember bad events or bad people. But here is another wonderful advantage of age: the bad doesn't seem quite so bad as it once did. The bad may even seem funny.

There was a certain person in my life about forty years ago whom at the time I hated. Or if I didn't hate him, at least I was unnerved by him, made miserable by him. Occasionally he still comes to mind. I cannot blot him out completely. But, wonder of wonders, he now amuses me.

"How could I have ever been upset by him?" I ask myself. "He was a blowhard, a vain little ass. He wasn't worth giving a second thought to."

If he is still alive, and he was such a tough customer that I am sure he is, he probably thinks these same things about me, and wonders why I ever annoyed him, as I no doubt did. He probably chuckles about me now, as I chuckle about him.

"That goofy little Armour guy," he thinks. "I shouldn't have wasted my time on him, needling him the way I did. But it was kind of fun, cutting him down and just about giving him apoplexy."

Come to think of it, the fellow I have in mind was several years younger than I. He may not yet have reached my age of wisdom, maturity, philosophic calm, perspective, etc. That "etc." is the most important part. It represents all of the things I am too modest to say about myself.

This leads me to mention another advantage of growing old. One does not worry so much as when young about being thought immodest or being thought anything. Speaking for myself, and I think I am also speaking for others of us oldsters, I now say just about anything I want to say, and to anyone and under any circumstances. Also I care much less than I once did about what people say about me.

It's not that I don't care about people's feelings, or that I have no feelings myself. In fact I think I feel more deeply about others than I once did, and my ego is still right in there, along with my super-ego and id and all the rest of my psyche. But the years have a way of building what I prefer to think of as confidence rather than callousness. For good or ill, we have become what we are and what we are likely to continue being for our remaining years. When you get to this point, it takes more than an unflattering remark to shake you. And as for the things you say—well, people make allowances for your age.

In this connection, something I read may interest you. It interested me enough to cause me to write a piece of verse about it. This is what I read: "Researchers have discovered that the skin becomes thinner with age, its thickness declining about half between the ages of 20 and 80." And this, called "Skin Game," is what I wrote:

Who was it coined the term "thin-skinned"?
On whom can such a thing be pinned?
They called me thin-skinned in my youth,
And I admit it was the truth,

And yet my skin was then much thicker,
Back when I flared up at a snicker.

They mostly call me "thick-skinned" now,
For I've grown callous as a cow.
If you'd insult me, you would find
There isn't much, now, that I mind.
I'm slow to anger, always calm;
To rouse me it would take a bomb.

Yet I've discovered that my skin
Is half as thick—it's very thin.
And so the terms "thin-skinned" and "thick"
No longer really seem to stick,
Or in old age that's known as ripe
I am a thick-skinned thin-skinned type.

There is one more advantage of growing old. If you are like me, you care less and less about how you look, which includes what you wear. A woman may buy a new dress now and then, but by the time she is seventy or so she has become sensible enough not to worry about keeping up with the latest fad, whether it be the height of heels or the length of hemline.

I have been told that the last part of a woman's body to age is the legs, so that whether the hemline is above, at, or below the knees might still be worth thinking about. I confess I have thought about it.

As for the man over seventy, he is even less concerned about keeping up with the latest fashion. A new tie now and then is enough for a change of pace, or of face. It saves money. It also saves time —all that deciding which outfit to wear.

I myself wear my son's cast-off clothes, the things that went out of style a couple of seasons ago. His sleeve length is 34, while mine is 33, but that is easily fixed. His shoes are somewhat larger than mine, but by wearing two pairs of heavy sox I can get by. If I wobble a bit, people are sympathetic.

"Poor old fellow," they say. "He probably won't be able to get around much longer."

Sometimes I jog a little, to throw them off.

I am wearing my son's shirt, tie, and shoes at this very moment, which means that I am only about two years behind the current styles. But I am wearing my own suit, which I bought twelve years ago, and it is beginning to have a mod look. The more styles change, the more they remain the same, to misquote the famous French aphorism.

These are only a few of the advantages of growing old. You can probably add many others.

Don't you feel sorry, now, for those immature, self-conscious, bewildered young people under sixty? The only thing that keeps them from being really depressed is that they don't know what they are missing.

6.

Getting Exercised About It

One good thing about getting along in years is that no one expects you to have muscles. If you do, you can make a display of them or not, just as you wish. I have referred to my penchant for pushups (not only floor pushups but chair pushups), the result of which is over-developed triceps. They do me no good whatsoever, since I have been told that triceps are chiefly useful to discus throwers, and I have never once had the occasion or the desire to throw a discus.

However since these are the only outstanding muscles I have, I make the most of them.

"Feel my triceps," I am likely to say to an utter stranger, who is usually happy to oblige, perhaps never having had such a request before.

Of course I twist my arm slightly and bunch up my triceps just before offering them to be felt. Unless I do this, they really aren't noteworthy.

"Ummm," the feeler will probably say. "How do you keep them so firm?"

This gives me a chance to do a few pushups (about as many as I can manage) and thus to elicit additional admiring comments.

But triceps are the only muscles in which I can and do take pride. In other areas, which I do not offer for feeling by strangers or even close friends, I am about what is expected of a person of my age. In other words, flabby.

Instead of being abnormal and something to be ashamed of, as would be the case with a young person, this is quite normal. If I am a little large around the waist, if I don't stand up ramrod straight, if my arthritic neck cracks when I turn it quickly, this is about what is expected. To be otherwise would mark me out among my contemporaries as a little odd, a physical-fitness buff or something of the sort.

So I should like to say one thing at the outset about exercise for anyone my age or older: it is up to each individual, preferably coached by a doctor rather than by an all-knowing neighbor.

Though it is better, both physically and psychologically, to be active rather than sedentary, in your later years you are free to set your own pace. Walk five miles a day if you wish to and are up to it, or one mile, or around the block—or lie back in your contour chair and watch TV. No longer are you on an athletic scholarship and honor bound to get out there and win. No longer are you worried whether you will perform up to the expectations of your fans.

As for worrying, I know one man of seventy-two who worries about not worrying.

"There must be something wrong with me," he says. "My son worries about his job and my granddaughter worries about her grades in school. But, frankly, I haven't a worry in the world."

This same man doesn't worry about overeating, since he enjoys food, and he doesn't worry about not having triceps like mine, which he probably thinks grotesque in a man of my age.

As for exercising, what he exercises is his freedom of choice not to exercise. He doesn't exercise one slightest bit. He would rather sit and read a good book, or even a bad book. Of course he may have overdeveloped eye muscles, rivaling my triceps, but he has never asked me to feel them.

If I suggest that he go for a walk, he pulls out of his file an article telling how many pedestrians are run over each year. If I suggest that he try lawn bowling, he shows me the obituary notice of a friend of his who had a heart attack while on the bowling green. It may have been the strenuous exercise or it may have been the excitement of a close game that did him in.

Did I say this fellow never exercises? I must admit he does the equivalent of a fair amount of calisthenics bending over to get something out of his files and straightening up, triumphantly, to show it to me. His waist measurement is smaller than mine, and this may be why. (Or it may be those genes, again.)

I have a friend, just turned seventy-five, who plays a good game of tennis. He has conceded that his doctor may be right, however, and lately limits himself to doubles. I also know a man and his wife, both well up in their seventies, who spend every Sunday hiking in the mountains over rough terrain and at high altitudes. They go to church first, though, which may be why they make it. These energetic people belt out the hymns in such a way that I have become persuaded that either (1) their hiking gives them the lungpower to sing so lustily or (2) singing the hymns provides them with the lungpower they need for hiking. I am not sure what the church service does for their legs. As Protestants, they don't get the calisthenic benefits of genuflection.

I am aware of people over a hundred who do phenomenal feats (or feets) of running, having seen them on TV. But you will have to admit that they are exceptional—else they would not have been on TV. If only someone could lead two lives, in one being sedentary during the later years and in the other jogging and lifting weights right to the end, we could be more certain than some of us are now about the benefits of exercise in old age. In this connection, I remind you of the old story about Cleopatra: how two skeletons were found of her, one as a girl and one as a mature woman.

Walking is of course the basic, universal exercise

and the one that most of us oldsters find the easiest
to accomplish. I take that back, if by walking you
think I meant, as I did, to walk upright on your two
feet. If you believe in the Darwinian theory of evo-
lution, man's ancestors walked on all fours, and
therefore that is perhaps the most basic and ele-
mentary exercise of all.

Indeed, I came across the following news item
not long ago: "A physical education expert says
that one of the best relaxing exercises is to get down
and walk around on all fours for a few minutes."
This item inspired (if that is the right word) the
following lines, entitled "Back to Nature":

> All right, to get in better shape
> I'll emulate the bear or ape
> And walk around (at least indoors)
> As best I can, upon all fours.
>
> Although perhaps I'll find it taxing,
> I'm told it's really quite relaxing
> And certainly no harder than
> Deep-knee bends for a creaking man,
>
> Or doing chins upon a bar
> And puffing (and without cigar),
> Or lifting dumbbells shoulder high
> (Or slightly less, upon the sly).
>
> So here I come, down on the floor—
> My feet, instead of two, are four.
> I hope that this of tension frees me,
> And also that nobody sees me.

But to return to walking, not on all fours but on all twos, or toes. The advantage of walking as compared with table tennis or shuffleboard or billiards or bowling is that you get around. You see places and people. Some people you may wish to avoid, but most you will be happy to see. You may even stop and talk a few minutes, which gives you a chance both to rest and to pick up the latest gossip.

I like walking, and at a brisk pace, but I prefer walking on a woodsy trail, or even just plain dirt, to walking on a sidewalk. Yet it is a sidewalk on which I walk, there being nothing else available nearby. My son's shoes, which I mentioned earlier, have thick rubber soles, and these take up some of the harsh impact of walking on cement. But I especially like walking on leaves, giving one a kick now and then and doing something useful as I help turn those I trample on into mulch.

It occurs to me that it would be nice to walk on grapes, making wine the while.

Dogs, I find, are no respecters of age. You might think my fringe of white hair and my slight stoop would keep them from running after me, snarling and baring their vicious teeth. The opposite is true. They are accustomed to the young people with whom they play, and no doubt I appear strange. Anything strange is to be attacked or at least frightened away.

I have never yet been attacked by a dog while walking, but I frighten easily, as dogs seem to know. I freeze in place. I speak soothing words. I hope the owner will hear the barking and call off his dogs. I pray. One thing I pray is that the owner of the dogs will learn about the leash law. Alas, he probably knows about it but thinks it a silly regulation, or one intended to apply only to others. His dogs can't be kept cooped up all the time, and if an old fellow insists on walking by he must take the consequences, which can range from a heart attack to a bite out of his leg. I am not sure which is worse.

Walking may be a good, normal exercise for the older person, but it is the possibility of an encounter with a friend, or with an unfriendly dog, that adds spice, if spice is what you like.

Bicycling is advocated by Dr. Paul Dudley White and others as being good for the heart and lungs. Besides, a bite from a dog can be avoided, if you are chased after, by placing the feet on the handlebars and coasting out of danger. However, any elderly person who is agile enough to place his feet on the handlebars and coast out of danger might as well work out on a trapeze or do something more spectacular than merely pedal a bike.

Swimming is fine, if the water is kept at around 90°. Even then, though youngsters think it far too warm (they like it around 72°), we older types have to ease into the water and shudder a while until we become accustomed to it. The ideal water temperature is 98.6°, dropping down to about 90° after you have been in a few minutes and done some moving around. However, it has been difficult, in my experience, to find a swimming pool with this sort of adjustable temperature.

Jogging is something you need to work up to. I have settled upon what I consider a healthful compromise. What I do is to alternate walking and jogging. I remember from Boy Scouts what was called "Scout's pace," which meant fifty running and fifty walking. My variation on this is twenty-five jogging and seventy-five walking. It's not quite as fast as Scout's pace, but it gets me there and, more important, it gets me back.

Golf is highly recommended, especially if you have a golf cart and need only drive up close to the ball and take a swing at it. When I was young, golf carts had not yet been invented, or had not come into use, and it was necessary to walk from tee to green, or from tee to rough to fairway to rough to fairway to green, meanwhile carrying a heavy bag of clubs—unless you could afford a caddie, which I couldn't. But nowadays golf is excellent for the quickly tired elderly who belong to a country club or can pay the greens fees at a municipal course.

I have heard of golfers in their seventies who could "shoot their age." That means a golfer aged seventy-six could shoot a 76, which isn't easy. It is hard enough for a golfer who is sixty-seven to shoot an 87, as well as to have good enough hearing to hear someone yell "Fore!" and quick enough reflexes to turn around and bend over and thus get hit on the buttocks instead of in the forehead.

I have sometimes wished I could "shoot my age" in the sense of shooting it with a shotgun and blowing it to smithereens. Then I would start off, on the golf course or wherever, with a brand-new age and none of my present handicaps.

The one thing golf takes, aside from money, is time, and time is what retired people have plenty of. The golf lover, now retired, is at last able to play seven days a week if he wants to. And if he has a home adjoining a golf course, ideally only a short walk from the first tee, he may be as close to Heaven as he will ever get.

Most retirement homes are equipped with indoor bowling greens, shuffleboards, and stationary bicycles with a cyclometer to indicate how far you have gone without going anywhere. These and other physical therapy conveniences make it unnecessary to go outdoors and risk the dogs or the chilly air. The most interesting contraption is the treadmill.

I know a man and his wife, both of them in their eighties, who love exercising on a treadmill. First he will tread a while and then she will, each keeping close account of the distance walked. What they really need is a treadmill built for two, so that they could walk side by side, or he a little ahead of her, as they do when they walk outdoors.

The treadmill, however, has bad connotations for me. I recall (not from personal experience but from reading) Sisyphus's eternal task of rolling a huge stone to the top of a high hill, only to have the stone roll back just as he reached the top. He would have to begin all over again, and his task was never finished. It was good exercise, but unproductive.

Sisyphus, I should point out, performed this stone-rolling stunt, or stint, not in a retirement home but in Hades, and it was Pluto who set him the task and kept him at it. Some retirement homes have a Physical Education Director, but the residents don't have to do what he tells them to do, no matter how much he wheedles and cajoles.

Once again, freedom is one of the most precious concomitants of the post-retirement years—freedom from work, freedom from worry, freedom from responsibility, freedom from being bossed by anyone other than your spouse, if you are lucky enough to have one.

So use your own judgment about what kind of exercise you do, and how much, if you do any at all. If, at your age, you haven't judgment, you still aren't old enough.

To conclude this treatment or mistreatment of the subject of this chapter:

"What do you do for exercise?"
I'm asked, but the question you'd see
If you looked in my mind would, I think, be this:
"What does exercise do for me?"

7.

Sex and the
Senior Citizen

I f I had used the title of this chapter as the title of my book, I might have had a best seller. It is not only the title that is intriguing, with its suggestion of intrigues, but it is the alliteration. Try saying it over and over to yourself, reveling in the sound of all those sibilants. It is easier to enunciate than "She sells seashells at the seashore," and almost as meaningful.

In my first chapter, if you can remember that far back, I said a little about sex in the later years, quoting not from Dr. Reuben but from John Heywood's *Proverbs* and the *Guinness Book of World Records*. I am not going to say a great deal more, partly because I want this book to be sold over the counter and partly because there is not a great deal more to say. But I have a few thoughts to pass along.

By the time you are in your sixties, seventies, or eighties, you have one advantage over the teenager whose sex drive is just getting into high gear. You know all about it, or at least you think you do. The teenager is still in the experimental stage, and still wondering and worrying.

"Is this the way to do it?" thinks one teenager.

"Is this all there is to it?" thinks another.

"Is it good for my health?" thinks still another, or maybe "Will it stunt my growth?"

But the senior citizen thinks no such worrisome thoughts. The sex drive may have eased back from high gear to intermediate, or even to low, but it is still there, at least psychologically. No need to smuggle books and pictures into the house and hide them under the mattress. No need to worry about what the principal will think if he finds out, and whether he will tell your mother and father.

The senior citizen can go to movies rated "PG," "R," or even "X" if he wants to.

The chances are that he won't want to. He has already seen it all, whether or not in the movies, and it's basically the same now as it was when he was young.

There is so much to remember, and no charge for admission: those first stories about the birds and the bees, the sophisticated boy, about a year older, who showed you the book, *How Babies Are Born,* out in the garage or behind the barn, and. . . . But I'll let you take over from there and do your own reminiscing.

You see, reminiscing is one of the greatest pleasures of sex, and you have to be fairly old before you have a good store of memories, unless you have lived what we used to call a "fast" life. When I say reminiscing is one of the greatest pleasures of sex, I mean (1) it lasts longer and (2) you can have it any time you want.

You don't need a bed, or another person. All you need is a chair to sit in while you let your mind wander. You can even do it while you are out walking, getting your exercise. In this respect it compares favorably with sex itself, which I have read is a form of exercise, using up I don't know how many calories. More than that, you don't even have to remember things that actually happened. You can imagine what *might* have happened. If sex is really important to you, more important than eating or watching your favorite program on TV, you can reminisce and/or imagine all day. That's another advantage of having plenty of time, now that you don't have to go to your job five days a week and try to keep your mind on your work, or pretend to, when a shapely young secretary saunters by.

But sex for the senior citizen doesn't have to be Walter Mittyish fantasy. It can be the Real Thing at an advanced age, as my earlier quotation from the *Guinness Book of World Records* indicates. When conditions are right and when the age is not too far advanced (i.e., over a hundred), there can be more satisfaction than ever. I know a couple in their mid-eighties about whom I can say this with some confidence and, by not telling their names, without betraying a confidence.

Thanks to a typographical error, which I quickly corrected, I first wrote their age not as "mid-eighties" but "mod-eighties." There might be a point here. My typewriter, which often acts as a separate entity, may have been trying to tell me something.

What I had in mind, however, is that this couple has one thing the very young don't have, or not to their degree, which is experience. And they have something else which is related to sex but above and beyond it, something that, if it is also the Real Thing, improves with age. I mean love.

The only trouble is that sex, or love, takes two. For some reason, perhaps because men do most of the work and the worrying, many women outlive their husbands. Fortunately I still have my wife. And fortunately (at least I hope she thinks so) she still has me. We have known each other since we were in first grade together, though we did not marry until somewhat later. Anyhow, it has been a long time, and yet it seems like a short time. When I say that love improves with age, I am speaking as an authority.

But I have been married only once. I am not envious, but I am curious, about those who have been married three or four times. Variety is the spice of life, but I am not sure it is the spouse of life. As for me, I'll take a lifetime spouse.

However, an eligible bachelor or widower seems

to get more and more eligible as the years go by. With more widows around, such an unattached (though not necessarily loose) person becomes not only eligible but edible, if you can tell anything from the hungry looks he gets.

My wife has always wanted to be a matchmaker. She has tried it many times, but succeeded only once. The man, once divorced and once widowed, was eighty-three. He was lonely, terribly lonely, and he appealed to my wife for help. I shall never forget one remark he made, as reported by my wife.

"I am capable of being a husband," he said, and my wife knew what he meant and so did I.

That was quite a few years ago, when such frankness about sex was not usual, especially coming from an octogenarian.

I am happy to say that my wife found a seventy-nine-year-old widow for him, and their blissful marriage lasted as long as they did, which was another ten years. My guess, and it is an educated guess based on not very subtle hints from the proud husband, is that their sex life, as well as their love life, also continued to the very end.

But how about the widower of seventy-five or eighty who enjoys his freedom? I mean the one who gets more thrill out of being pursued than being caught.

I have visited a number of retirement homes in different parts of the country and in each instance have made a check of the sex (not sex life) of the residents. Usually the women outnumber the men by about five to one. Some of the men are married and have their wives to keep them company, or to contend with. But there are also men who are single and thus available, or vulnerable. For better or worse, on a typical farm there is the even higher ratio of ten hens to one rooster.

At any rate, or ratio, the men in these retirement homes are like a little group of settlers of the old West, surrounded by Indians. Some are a little frightened, but most enjoy the contest. They are not flattened, they are flattered. No matter what they say, you can tell by their sly looks and smug smiles that they love it.

"Why don't you marry her?" I asked a man of seventy-eight who was obviously being pursued by an attractive woman in her upper sixties. She looked pretty sexy to me, and she had money too.

"I had a good marriage," he said. "I might not be as lucky the second time."

"She's at least ten years younger than you," I said, teasing him along, "and could pass for ten years younger than that. She has plenty of sex appeal."

He didn't say anything, but of all the broad leers I saw around that retirement home, his was the broadest. Finally he spoke up.

"There are romances all over the place," he said.

The word he used, and used several times afterward, was "romance." I didn't press him for a more specific term or a definition. Besides, I am old enough to like the old-fashioned word "romance" myself.

Maybe the title of this short chapter, in which I am leaving much unsaid, should be "Romance and the Senior Citizen." It would lose some of the alliteration, but it would gain a little nostalgia.

8.

Income and Outgo

Probably no piece of light verse I have ever written has been so much quoted as one that is on a subject that is of great importance to retired people and is the theme of this chapter. These lines have been set to music, made into a charm bracelet, and used in the fund-raising campaigns of such institutions as Harvard and the University of Toronto. I refer to the following:

MONEY

Workers earn it,
Spendthrifts burn it,
Bankers lend it,
Women spend it,
Forgers fake it,
Taxes take it,
Dying leave it,
Heirs receive it,
Thrifty save it,

Misers crave it,
Robbers seize it,
Rich increase it,
Gamblers lose it. . .
I could use it.

The fund-raisers, I might add, changed the last line to "*We* could use it."

There is a great difference in the attitude toward money in one's earlier years and in one's later years, or before and after retirement. In the earlier years the idea is to earn as much as possible in order to spend as much as possible. Those are the years of hard work, risk-taking, and good or bad luck, the years of moving up the socio-economic ladder, keeping up with the Joneses and ahead of the Smiths.

Goals include building or buying a bigger house in a nicer neighborhood, joining the country club, educating the children, owning two cars, traveling, entertaining, and supporting an incredible number of charities.

But gradually the goals change to a single goal: providing for the post-retirement years. "The last of life, for which the first was made" was Browning's way of putting it, but I would revise it to read "for which the money's made."

Some, in their later years, are "well-heeled." Or they may be "well-fixed." The former would suggest that they keep their money in their sock, thus explaining that slight limp. The latter would appear to indicate that they were once broke but whatever was broken has been so well repaired that you would never know it.

Occasionally some elderly person is spoken of as "loaded," which would be dangerous in the case of a pistol but is highly desirable when it comes to money.

Whether the person is well-heeled, well-fixed, or loaded, this status may have come about in any one or a combination of the following ways:

1. Many years of work for a company that has a generous retirement system, together with a stock option plan that has been advantageously used.

2. Good (i.e., shrewd or lucky) investments in stocks, land, or a business of some sort.

3. Inheritance. This can be from wealthy parents or from relatives who, fortunately, had no children of their own. Or, especially with women who have had several short-lived or divorced husbands, one or two of whom they married at least partly for their money, it can be what I would call matrimonial accretion.

By whatever means it was obtained, money is a nice thing to have after you have stopped earning it. The years of worrying about making more and more have passed. Now come the years of worrying about not having enough.

I should add that there is quite a difference between being well-fixed and being on a fixed income, especially in a time of inflation. (I seem to have a fixation on the word "fixed.")

One kind of fixed income is a pension, particularly one that doesn't have a cost-of-living clause built into it. Another kind of fixed income, though the government can keep fixing it up, is Social Security. The word "pension" goes back to the Latin *pensio,* a paying or payment, but what I like most about it is its being akin to the Latin *pendere,* meaning to hang. From this I have visions of a person on a pension who is either just hanging around or hanging on for dear life or even being hanged, slowly throttled economically.

As for Social Security, I find it a complete misnomer. There is nothing very social about it. And as for the security, well just ask anyone who has nothing but Social Security how secure he or she feels.

The ideal situation is to have income in the form of dividends, interest, rentals, a pension (or several pensions), *and* Social Security. I know some people who possess such a combination of inflowing money, and it is a joy to be around them. It is even more of a joy if they are such good, generous friends that they just can't do enough for you. They can try, though, and I for one am never heard to object.

I know of a couple in their upper eighties who have all of the above, and more. They live in a beautiful home, full of books and objects of art and expensive mementos from all over the world. They have a full-time gardener, a cook, and a house-keeper. They not only know where their next meal is coming from but whether it will include choice New York cut steak, prime ribs, or lobster tails. The wine is imported and a superb vintage.

They are obviously loaded and so, for a few hours, is anyone who has the good fortune to have dinner with them.

Man cannot live by bread alone, it is said, and people can't live like that on Social Security alone, or even with a small pension in addition.

These opulent octogenarians, I might add, give generously to many charities. I wish I had the nerve to suggest that their favorite charity might be me. I have gone so far as to say "I can take it," but they thought I referred to hardships, not hard cash.

More typical of the elderly is a cousin of my wife's. He has just enough income from invest-ments so that when this is added to his Social Security he "makes out pretty well." That is, he can splurge now and then on a new sweater or a box of candy. But he is always figuring it close.

"I'm shifting into bonds that pay seven and a half percent," he said once. "I was getting only seven percent on my utility stocks."

That extra one-half of one percent makes the difference between his living on the ragged edge and on the unragged edge.

We encourage him to go into his principal, and to have a good time.

"You have nothing to worry about," we tell him. "If you live another ten years" (which he keeps telling us he's sure he won't, but I'm not so sure he's sure) "you couldn't spend all your principal."

But he won't do it. He gives as his reasons the increase of prices, the possibilities of illness beyond coverage by Medicare, and something he refers to as his estate.

To some people an estate is a spacious piece of property, but to others, especially those along in years, an estate is a form of earthly immortality, something they leave behind them. What matter if those to whom the estate is left are getting along better financially than the elderly person who is barely subsisting? There is a curious sense of pride in leaving an estate that will be looked at respectfully and gratefully by the inheritors—and the lawyers and the IRS.

This cousin of my wife's, or actually cousin-in-law, has no children, no close relatives of his own, only some relatives of his deceased wife. They really don't need his money, but something—pride or stubbornness or satisfaction in self-sacrifice—causes him to deny himself in these last years of his life. He *must* leave an estate.

There is a way, of course, his sacrifices would not be in vain. He could leave that little old estate of his to us. I have dropped a few hints, as I have to the charitable friends I mentioned earlier. But I have seen his will, and the beneficiaries of his estate are all settled upon, and we are not included.

For one thing, we are too old. We should be worrying about our own estate, as he keeps telling us.

This man is completely different from a friend who is healthy and vigorous long past the time allotted by the actuarial tables. I have never once heard him mention the word "estate."

"I earned it and I'm going to spend it," he says. Of course by spending it on himself and living comfortably and having the very best medical care he may outlive those who were to have been his heirs. If they are not too happy about it, at least he brings joy to his insurance company, who expected to pay off on him at least ten years ago, and continue to get interest on what he has paid in for the past sixty years, as well as current premiums.

Not that he is stingy. He is very generous to his wife and his friends and his church. He simply believes that he who hath hath, and that those he begat can do a little getting, as well as begetting, for themselves. It's not a bad idea.

I am a middle-of-the-roader, and I long ago learned that the middle of the road is the best place for getting run over. To put it another way, I am always saying "On the one hand . . . but on the other," and wishing I had a third hand.

So, in my usual position, I am somewhere between the two persons I have cited above, both of whom are more definite and decisive than I am. If I have slightly overstated both cases, it has been to make a point, not to point a finger. Also I have probably been affected by one of my besetting sins, envy—in this instance envy of those who know what they are doing and why.

One way or another, and for the most part honestly, I hope in my non-worrying years to have enough money not to worry about income and outgo. I have always been known as the outgoing sort, but I should like to have ample incoming too.

But since I have a son and a daughter and some grandchildren, I think it would be nice to leave them what I have referred to above as an estate. The ideal will be not to deny myself and yet also not to deny them.

Still better, I hope I can help them, and others who need help, while I am around to get some satisfaction out of it. My wife feels even more strongly about this than I do. But then, my family came from Scotland. What we Scots earn, we hang onto. The term "scot-free," as you might guess, has no connection with Scot. The "scot" comes from the Anglo-Saxon word meaning to shoot, to contribute, and the noun is a sum of money assessed or paid, a tax. The very thought of a scot causes cold chills in a Scot.

With the passing years, though, I have learned that giving becomes easier. If I live long enough I may find I can do it with less and less pain and more and more pleasure. Meanwhile my wife is tutoring me.

In the so-called golden years, it is nice to have a little gold. But, unlike the earlier years, a little is enough. There are many different ways, not all of them self-centered, to enjoy whatever money you are fortunate enough to have.

Though I am old enough to have learned something about it, I still know very little about money —how to make it or what to do with it. A book that would appeal to me would be entitled *Yenom: Money for Backward People.*

So don't take this chapter too seriously, but take it.

9.

The Company You Keep Keeps You Company

There is that old saying, "Misery loves company." But it would be just as accurate, and even more applicable to senior citizenry, to make it "Happiness loves company" or "Company makes happiness." Most people like to be with people, and older people especially like not only to be active but to be with others who are active—or at least as active as they are. I prefer drop-ins to dropouts, and I have never known of a really jolly hermit.

Many have written depressingly about the loneliness of old age, but not enough has been said (so I propose to say it) about the fun of being with people who are fun to be with.

You can probably remember, as I can, all those years of being with people you honestly didn't care to be around, such as business associates who were above you and lording it over you or below you and trying to get your job. There were the people you "owed" socially and never had the time to pay back, perhaps because you didn't like them quite enough to find the time. There were also the people you felt you had to impress.

Now, at last, you are free of the whole parcel of them. You can concentrate on the people—few or many—who are a pleasure to be with. And you have the time to be with them and they have the time to be with you.

In your later years you cherish friends more than ever. Speaking for myself, and putting it in verse:

Old friends, I've heard it said, are best,
Which seems unfair to all the rest.
For instance, friends I've met just now
And all these years have missed somehow.
I couldn't help it, nor could they,
We didn't meet until today.
Friends old or new I find so great
I never check the starting date.

The best way to combine activity and the company of like-minded people, or people who like each other's minds, is to engage in a group activity. Over seventy, unless you are also over seven feet, you are not likely to organize a basketball team, though there would be no harm in practicing free throws with a group of ex-basketballers or those who always wanted to play basketball but were afraid to try it.

But you can make it big on the local lawn bowling team, perhaps even playing against the teams of other cities. A friend of mine, age seventy-two, is the best lawn bowler around, or so he tells me. In fact he can prove it with his case full of trophies, all of them won since he took up the game when he turned sixty-five and retired.

"What do you like most about lawn bowling?" I asked him. I thought he would mention the exercise, the fresh air, the feel of the turf underfoot, the sight of the ball rolling along and stopping where he wanted it to stop.

"What do I like about lawn bowling?" he mused. "I like my partner. I like the whole crowd, including those who simply watch and applaud the good shots. I like being a member of the team. Best of all, I like being captain of the team, which I've been for two years."

If there is such a thing as modest pride, he has it.

"How often do you bowl?" I asked him.

"Every day," he said. "Unless it rains. Then I play gin rummy or poker or pool with the same fellows. They're a great bunch."

I know an elderly elder in our church who has never impressed me as being very religious, and yet he is what is known as "a pillar of the church." He sleeps through the sermons, and there are those who say his heavy breathing distracts them.

Yet how he loves to take up the collection and greet people at the end of the service. He is wide awake then.

"Fine sermon, wasn't it?" he says, not having heard a word of it.

He serves on innumerable committees and belongs to all sorts of discussion groups. If anything is going on at the church, he is there; in fact he probably organized it.

He may be doing all this for the Lord. The Lord only knows, I don't. But whatever other motives he may have, he obviously likes to be around people and to have people around him. Those who knew him before he retired, when he was "all business," say he was very different. He was rather aloof, a loner. But something happened to him. He has found what he had been too busy for—people. He can hardly wait until Sunday. Anyone who has had his hand shaken by my friend on the way out of church feels as if he had grasped a high-tension electric wire.

I mentioned the man who made his friendships through lawn bowling. How do women do it?

Women are more gregarious than men, I think, and when they no longer have a husband to look out for, or even if they do, they tend to gather together and revel in one another's company. The game they seem to enjoy most is bridge.

Bridge is well named. It is a bridge, or a chain of bridges, that brings people together in close proximity. There are no walls in bridge, except maybe the back of a hand of cards which one would like to peek over. There is ample opportunity to talk while cards are being dealt and scores are being tallied and, for those who never stop talking, during the play. Oddly named, the dummy is least likely to be dumb—that is, voiceless.

As I write this, my wife is having a bridge party, it being her turn to have "her club" at our house. There are three tables, which I helped set up, and a total of twelve ladies. From as much as I can hear of the talk, two rooms away, everyone is having a good time. The gossip is flying, or flowing. Even those with poor hands seem to be enjoying themselves, which is another indication that it isn't the game but the companionship that is fun.

Almost my only quarrel with my wife is that she plays bridge too much.

"You play bridge every day," I tell her. "And four or five hours at a stretch."

"I don't either," she retorts. "At most only once a week, and you know we never play more than about three hours."

She is probably right. It only *seems* to me that she plays so often and so long. If I played bridge too, and were permitted to join her exclusive all-woman club, I might have a different attitude.

"Bridge is a complete waste of time," I tell her.

"It sharpens the mind," she says. "It keeps you alert." And then comes her clincher. "Besides, I like it."

What she really likes, I know, is the people she plays bridge with, the members of her club. They are a little like members of a sorority. It isn't easy to get in, and there is pride in being included.

I doubt that being a good bridge player counts as much as having a pleasant personality.

Sometimes when I say "Bridge is a complete waste of time," she has another rejoinder.

"It's *my* time," she says. "I can do anything I want to with it. And that includes wasting it."

Since time is something you have more of, or more at your own disposal, in the later years, I am unable to dispute her statement. In fact I agree that one of the pleasantest things to do with time (but not all the time) is to waste it.

However, I do wish that bridge, as well as other card games, could be played with weighted cards. Each card might be made of lead, or it might be pulled downward by a magnetized table. Then at least the card player would get some exercise and improve the muscle tone of the fingers and forearms.

If you have never before thought of bridge in connection with physical fitness, this might start you thinking about it. Perhaps I should hasten to take out a patent for a card game that would replace weights and calisthenics. It could be called Heavy Bridge or Healthy Bridge or Calisthenic Cards.

Group activity is often the continuation of a hobby. Painters take their easels to some scenic spot and with fellow artists sketch the landscape, ohing and ahing at each other's masterpieces. Picasso kept painting until his death at the age of ninety-one. Michelangelo was still at it when he was eighty-nine, though he had turned from painting and sculpture to architecture in his last years.

Such geniuses probably worked alone, or with assistants, but the ordinary minor artist or hobbyist likes companionship. Friends are made in a painting or ceramics class, or a writing class, or a sewing class. As the art progresses, so does the friendship. There is no greater act of friendship than to admire a work of art just because you know and like the person who created it.

"I wish I could draw like that" when said to someone whose work you consider inferior to your own may be the result of friendship, ineptness as a critic, or sheer hypocrisy. But if it makes the other person feel better. . . .

I have heard of those who go so far as to purchase the art works of their friends.

Recently I saw (and heard) on TV a group of retirees, some of them well over eighty, who had formed an orchestra. How they were blowing and fiddling and banging away! They might never get an engagement in Carnegie Hall, but they were having a great time together. It was a good example of keeping up with a hobby and doing something with others. You can't, or had better not, go your own way in an orchestra.

I think the members of this group were having more fun than the members of a professional orchestra. Some were watching the conductor and some, leaning over close to the music, were not. They could hit a sour note now and then, or forget to come in when they should, without losing their job. Of course they tried their best, but they also knew that their best was all that was expected of them, no matter what their best was.

On this same TV program I saw some elderly couples dancing. They were dancing waltzes, polkas, and fox trots, and doing very well at it. I saw no one's toes stepped on, saw no expressions of pain. Everyone was smiling, or looking dreamy. Perhaps the men were imagining they were Fred Astaire, dancing with Ginger Rogers, while the women were imagining they were Ginger Rogers, dancing with Fred Astaire.

Lawrence Welk has proved that there is no age limit to dancing. Moreover, dancing of the old-fashioned kind, where there is body contact, is more companionable than the solo gyrations of the young rock-and-rollers.

After years of putting up with the single dance step I did, the so-called box step or square step (which marked me as a square indeed), my wife finally prevailed upon me to take a course of lessons with her at a dancing school. As I recall, we were lured into it by some sort of special offer or coupon. We kept on with it even after the original course ran out, which is what they had hoped. It may have been the dancing instructor assigned to me who kept me at it. She looked a little like Raquel Welch, and when I put my arms around her she felt as I presume Raquel feels.

"Don't watch your feet," she kept telling me.

I wasn't watching my feet, though I must admit

I was looking down. She wore a very low-cut dress.

My wife and I got pretty good at dancing, for people of our age or of any age, and soon were doing all the fancy steps, being especially proud of our tango.

If *I* can dance, in fact if I can lead, being as un-leading a type as you will ever come across, anyone can do it. I recommend dancing to anyone who, at whatever age, wants fun, exercise, companionship, and dreams.

Especially companionship and dreams.

10.

Getting Away from It All

Now that you have the time, and assuming you also have the money, you can travel. Travel broadens, and if you aren't broad enough already, here is your chance.

"What are you going to do when you retire?" is the inevitable question, usually the first one put to anyone who is nearing retirement age.

"Well, I suppose we'll do a little traveling" is the answer that comes back nine times out of ten.

The question to ask then is "Where?" or "When?" or "How long?" If it is a relative or someone you know really well, it may be "How much do you think it will cost?"

Most people have been planning where and how they will travel for many months, perhaps many years. That is the best part of travel, or at least the safest, most comfortable, and least expensive. It is the time to read history books and travel guides and to study maps and to ask those who have been there.

However I'll wager that not many prepare themselves by reading Francis Bacon's essay *Of Travel*. The very first sentence applies beautifully to our present subject. "Travel, in the younger sort," says Bacon, "is a part of education; in the elder, a part of experience." In other words, the young person travels (as in the present junior year abroad at colleges) to learn—if possible picking up transferable credits.

He should already have some knowledge of foreign languages, according to Bacon, and should travel with a tutor who will tell him "what things are worthy to be seen ... what acquaintances to seek ... and what exercises or discipline the place yieldeth." If he doesn't have such preparation and guidance, says Bacon, he will "go hooded" and see little.

Bacon's whole essay is only three pages, and I am tempted to quote all of it so that you will not miss a word of its wisdom, its loftiness, and for the average traveler today, of whatever age, its impracticability.

Bacon believes in keeping a diary, which is still good advice, but he would keep a record of *everything*, which would include descriptions of the courts of princes, the courts of justice, consisteries ecclesiastic, churches and monasteries, walls and fortifications, havens and harbors, antiquities and ruins, armories, arsenals, exchanges, burses, warehouses, treasuries of jewels and robes, cabinets and rarities, and "whatsoever is memorable."

He also urges making the acquaintance of ambassadors and seeing and visiting "eminent persons in all kinds, which are of great name abroad." This was apparently easier to arrange in the late sixteenth and early seventeenth centuries than today, though name-dropping is still a pleasant pastime of the returned traveler.

Most of the above applies to travel by the young, seeking education. Fortunately, not so much is expected of us older people, traveling merely to add to a lifetime of experience. So you who are over sixty-five can relax when you read Bacon's *Of Travel*. Keep a diary if you wish, visit the armories and arsenals if you wish, meet the eminent personages if you can—or go shopping or have a leisurely drink in a sidewalk café, where you may learn as much about the life of the country as anywhere.

Bacon has nothing to say about which hotels and eating places are the best bargains, how much to tip, and the many other things of primary importance to most of us. Anyhow, prices were probably somewhat different in 1597, when the first edition of his *Essays* was published. He doesn't even mention the problems of baggage, succinctly stated as follows about 370 years later:

Here is a strange, rather eerie fact,
A thought that is certain to haunt:

How bags can contain twice as much as you need
Yet lack half the things you want.

Of course you may not go abroad. You may make
a trip by car or bus or plane or train around the
United States, going where it is scenic or salubrious
or where you have friends (good friends indeed) or
relatives with whom you can stay.

But travel, to many who have retired, means
going by plane or ship to Europe or Asia or Africa
or somewhere your friends have been or, better yet,
where they have not been. It means many things
blissfully unknown to Bacon, such as typhoid and
tetanus shots (better than getting typhoid or tetanus, at that), passport photos (which you are un-
likely to frame), visas, traveler's checks, and, on
arrival back in your home country, going through
customs.

When I was young, I took parties of tourists to
Europe for six summers. These were "personally
conducted tours," of which I was both conductor
and motorman, ballyhooing on buses, lecturing in
museums, handling the baggage, assigning the
rooms, paying the bills, hurrying the late, and paci-
fying the quarrelsome. I had no time to keep a
diary, but I kept account of expenditures, else the
owner of the tour company would have taken any
unaccountable loss not only out of my pocket but
out of my hide.

I got an education, all right, but not so much in
art and history as in people, most of them thirty to

fifty years older than I. It did not take me long to learn the two things elderly tourists are most eager to find in an art museum: (1) the W.C. and (2) a place to sit down. Being aware of what was of greatest importance, I had these spotted before I knew for sure where the Mona Lisa was. If I do say so myself, I was a very popular tour leader and guide.

I have been back to some of these museums in my own post-sixty-five period, and have discovered to my great satisfaction that I still know where to find the aforementioned essentials in the Louvre, the Uffizi, and the British Museum. It assists and impresses my companions more than anything I can tell them about the Venus de Milo or the Winged Victory of Samothrace.

In the preceding chapter I mentioned the enjoyment of people in people, in companionship, especially as they grow older. For those who can afford it, travel on some sort of a tour, with a group, is about the quickest way to get to know people and often to turn companions into friends.

"Where are you going next?" I ask some of our travelingest acquaintances.

"The Greek islands," they say, or "the Scandinavian countries," or "Japan." Or maybe "the South Seas and Australia."

"Are the Nelsons going with you again?" I ask.

"Of course," they say. "We wouldn't go without them."

They didn't know the Nelsons until they made that charter tour of Austria, Switzerland, and the

Italian Lakes, followed by the Mediterranean cruise. But now the Nelsons are their closest friends.

You can make enemies, too, on tours, but in a group of twenty or thirty the few unpleasant people can be easily avoided. I remember during my tour-leader days there was a very difficult old lady whom no one else would eat with. So, to spare others, I ate every meal with her, at a table for two. I was getting paid for it, and I always kept a few digestive pills in my pocket.

It is on trips with just two families that instead of making friends you can lose them. Here is one way of putting it:

Say you and your wife take a trip with friends,
Old friends and the dearest of dear.
Two weeks or a month, from morning till night,
You're always together or near.

The first day is fine. The second's so-so.
The third, things begin to go sour.
By the end of a week you are thinking of mayhem
And counting each passing hour.

At last you get home. Oh, that happy day
When you stand on your Welcome mat.
Your trip is finished at last, but your friendship
Was finished some time before that.

However, this doesn't happen often, and it is worth the risk. People who travel together are usually happy together. They are relaxed, for one thing, and on their best behavior.

Where people come together best is on a cruise,

where they are in a confined, but not too confined, space together for days, weeks, even months. There is no hustle and bustle of changing planes at airports and getting to hotels and leaving hotels and boarding buses and all the rest, and unrest, of it.

A leisurely cruise might not seem exciting to young people, except maybe for a young woman in search of a man who is unattached and has the time and money to travel instead of work and may, indeed, be in search of a wife. But for older people a cruise is great, without exception. It's easy living, even luxurious living, with plenty of people somewhat like you close at hand. The only trouble may be overeating, but with shuffleboard and deck tennis and brisk walks around the deck this can be compensated for. Or go ahead and gain a few pounds and lose them later.

Important also, for people our age, there is a medical unit on board, including a competent doctor and a couple of attentive nurses.

Best of all, there are no twinges of conscience. The retired person doesn't have to worry about how the business is getting along without him. As a matter of fact the firm may have given him this cruise in recognition of his many years of faithful service.

Could it be that they wanted him to keep from dropping into the office and making suggestions?

There are those who travel a moderate amount and those who are planning another trip even while they are on one.

I know someone in the latter category. I see him only briefly, between trips. He and his wife, both of them in their late seventies, have been everywhere, or everywhere worth going to. But still they go. Sometimes they go where they haven't been for as long as two years, such as Salzburg or Lake Como. Sometimes they take a tour to one of the rare places they have somehow missed, such as Mindanao or Sierra Leone.

Always they return with three or four hours of slides, mercifully cut down to an hour and a half. Their excellent photos of scenery, festivals, shrines, and themselves enable their friends to see the world with no effort and no expense, and these evenings of slides-and-narration fill in their own time until they are off again.

Francis Bacon, in addition to being a writer, was something of a scientist. As you probably know, he died at the age of sixty-five, barely making it to senior citizenship. He might have lived longer but became ill during an experiment with refrigeration, when he tried to stuff a chicken with snow instead of bread crumbs and seasoning.

And yet, despite all of his talents, Bacon never thought of inventing photography, or he could have added an interesting paragraph or two to the essay with which I began this chapter.

One final word about travel and travelers. There are those, with the time and money to be forever on the go, who give a curious reason for their incessant travel.

"To get away from it all," they say. They could be curious, or they could be restless. But the fact is that they are always happy to come back. As for getting away from it all, that is impossible. They never succeed in getting away from themselves.

This should be some consolation to those who, for whatever reason, physical or financial, have to stay home. No one can really get away from it all, in the fullest sense of the word, and very few really want to.

The expression "get with it" has been preempted by youth, but it applies to all ages. Maybe, with travel, it should be slightly altered to "get it and come back with it."

So travel if you wish, and enjoy yourselves. Or stay home and watch your friends' travel films. The only people more popular than those who are willing to sit through other people's travel films are those who stay awake while watching them.

11.

Audio-Visual Matters

Of the five physical senses, three hold up wonderfully well as one grows old. I refer to touch, smell, and taste. A sixth sense, the sense of humor, also stays in good shape to the very last. It is a little like a muscle, though, and it develops with use and atrophies from lack of use.

I had the pleasure of reviewing P. G. Wodehouse's ninetieth book, published on the author's ninetieth birthday. The creator of Jeeves was as funny and inventive as ever. Here was a nonagenarian who could not only appreciate but create humor.

Two of the physical senses, however, give some of us a little trouble as we get along in years: sight and hearing. Let me start out with sight, the sense that most of us prize above all. I would hate not to be able to hear or taste or smell (though sometimes I would be happy if this sense were not quite so acute) or touch. But I would trade all four of these senses, if I had to, for the ability to see.

Luckily, someone invented glasses. It was probably a Chinese, as early as 500 B.C. Marco Polo reported that he saw many Chinese wearing glasses when he went on his famous journey to the Orient in the late thirteenth century. Whether Marco Polo himself wore glasses, picking up a pair in Peking, I do not know, but he lived to be about seventy (there is some question about his birth and death dates), and thus reached the age when glasses have long since been useful, if not essential, to most of us.

Since I do not know the name of the Chinese inventor, if you wish to thank someone for making it possible for you to read (in addition to Gutenberg), I suggest Roger Bacon. He included much information about spectacles in his *Opus Majus*, published in 1268, sixteen years before he died at the age of eighty. If you wish to say a little prayer for the inventor of bifocals, mention the name of Benjamin Franklin. He had plenty of time to experiment with lenses and refraction, living to be eighty-four.

I have indicated my personal indebtedness to everyone concerned with the invention, perfection, and fitting of glasses in these lines:

> Increasingly, each day that passes,
> I'm grateful that I have my glasses.
> Without them I'd not see the view,

Nor would I view the sea, it's true.
I could not read the daily paper
About the latest captious caper.
I could not watch TV and find
Commercials that would lift my mind.
I would not see a step, or bomb,
Nor could I be a Peeping Tom.
I'd get along without my teeth,
The ones above, the ones beneath.
I'd get along without my shoes—
They'd really not be much to lose.
But without glasses, nothing visible,
I must confess that I'd be misible!

Give thanks, then, to Benjamin Franklin, Roger Bacon, and all the others who are responsible for these remarkable aids to vision, these adjuncts to the most important of our five senses. Actually I have myself gone beyond bifocals to trifocals, and may get to quadrifocals if they are available.

Frankly, I am envious of those who are my age or older but can read without glasses. My wife both amazes and annoys me. She is seven months older than I am (though she is often taken for seven years younger), and yet uses her glasses rarely. She can see better with them, but she can do remarkable things without them.

Sometimes I come home and find her in the almost-dark, reading the newspaper or even looking up a number in the phone book—without her glasses. You see (and maybe you see better than I do), she has been sitting there while the day waned, and her eyes somehow adjusted to the lessening light. It reminds me of the man who lifted a baby calf, and then lifted the creature each day until it was a full-grown cow. Gradualness does it, I guess.

I turn on the light, partly because I think reading in the dark must be bad for my wife's eyes and partly because I am envious of her eye muscles, optic nerves, sheer determination, or whatever it is she has that I haven't.

I like to tell people that she doesn't wear her glasses because she is afraid that looking through them will wear out the lenses. Sometimes this gets a laugh, which gives me a little satisfaction. But I am still envious.

My chief trouble with glasses, as I get older and more forgetful, is finding them.

"Where are my glasses?" I ask my wife.

"Wherever you left them," she answers helpfully.

Glasses can be left in a remarkable number of places. Once I sat on a pair I had left on my bed. Luckily, only the frames broke. Otherwise I would have needed not only lenses but some painful surgery. When I am able to find my glasses, I am often unable to find my glasses case. What a great feeling it is, after looking all over, to discover that my glasses are on my face and my glasses case is in my coat pocket. Any such rare occasion of total victory will make my day for me. I have been known to burst into song or whistle merrily, overcome by relief and joy.

Before I leave the subject of glasses, let me quote something I wrote soon after I got my first bifocals:

> Bifocals help so very much,
> I see things, now, so plain,
> I wish I could get fitted with
> A gadget for my brain.
>
> I'd go to my brainologist,
> My memory he'd test.
> My judgment, too, he'd check with care,
> For it's not at its best.
>
> Then, fitted with a brain device
> And paying without blinking,
> I'd confidently face the world
> With 20/20 thinking.

I may not have 20/20 thinking yet, but as I get older I become more and more convinced that I have 20/20 hindsight. Once again it is a matter of time. I have more behind me to think about and more time to think about what I should have done instead of what I did. But if my present glasses don't help me fix up my errors of the past, they help me see the present more clearly—at least the scribbled letters from our daughter and the front step that I was always tripping over. I am very grateful.

And now for the sense of hearing. For a long while I thought my hearing was perfectly good, and that people were just mumbling more than usual.

"I could hear a pin drop," I would say, "if they didn't make pins so light these days."

At my wife's insistence I went to an ear man, more professionally known as an otolaryngologist, and was convinced by the tests he put me through that I am indeed hard of hearing. I suppose the opposite of hard of hearing is soft of hearing, and I don't care for that idea either.

Apparently I can hear low sounds better than high sounds, which means that I should go to concerts featuring contraltos and basses rather than sopranos and tenors. And, in general, I should be in the company of men more than women. I also may have to give up listening to birds.

I can struggle along, with an occasional "Huh" or "Whuzzat?" Or I can join the fifteen million people in the United States who wear hearing aids.

Fortunately, it is no longer necessary to use an ear trumpet, such as I can recall my great-grandfather's using when I was a small boy. Experiments with hearing aids using bone conduction go back to the early seventeenth century, and ultimately Alexander Graham Bell invented a crude hearing aid. It is said that the telephone grew out of his efforts to contrive a hearing aid for his mother.

It was not until 1934, however, that an electric bone-conduction receiver was invented, and from that time forward the use of an electrical transmitter with ear receiver, something like a radio, has become commonplace. The device has now been perfected to the point that you can hardly see it, tucked in the ear or made into a part of one's glasses frame. Hearing aids are now much less noticeable than glasses, except for contact lenses.

Sydney Smith, the English essayist, once wrote: "Thank God for tea! What would the world do without tea? —how did it exist? I am glad I was not born before tea."

I like tea all right, but I could get along without it. What am I really glad I was not born before? Lots of things, including central heating and air conditioning and the automobile and the airplane and the typewriter and adhesive tape and anesthesia (which was first used in 1846, a year after Sydney Smith's death).

But I am happiest not to have been born so early that, when I needed them, I would have had to do without glasses (bifocals) and an inconspicuous hearing aid.

I have to keep reminding myself how lucky I am, in a chronological or historical sense. Maybe you should do this too. Science has come to the assistance of those of us who are having a little trouble with our sight and hearing. Thank you, science.

12.

A Short Course
in Medicine

I know what I want most as I grow older: good health. I would even settle for fairly good health. The human body is a marvelous contrivance, but it does get a bit frayed as time goes on. At that, it lasts far longer and takes fewer repairs than the finest automobile. Nor does it require the expensive upkeep—the roofing, repainting, replastering, as well as the repair of electrical and plumbing facilities—of a house that by human standards would be very young indeed.

"How are you?" is, with young people, not a question but a salutation, Or you might call it a rhetorical question, one that requires no answer. Some respond with an automatic "O.K." or "All right" or with a reciprocal "How are *you*?" to which no answer is expected. One "How are you?" for another "How are you?" is simply a social convention, a stalemate.

But when I ask friends who are my age or older,

"How are you?" or they ask it of me, it is a clinical question. An answer is expected and desired. The questioner is genuinely interested, and he is willing (and has the time) to listen to a detailed description of symptoms, prognoses, medication, and all the rest.

"How are you?" may be asked out of friendly, humanitarian interest—or there may be an element of selfishness in it. You see, the questioner may have, may have had, or may anticipate someday having whatever ailment the other person currently has. If you ask enough people, I have discovered, you will find someone who has the same trouble you have and has a doctor who prescribes something different from what is prescribed by your own doctor. It may be worth trying.

And what isn't worth trying? My wife, who is the daughter of an M.D., will try anything for the arthritis that afflicts her neck and thumbs. We have a closet full of devices that have been tried and found wanting. She wears a copper bracelet that does no good but looks rather attractive. She is the first person in our town to have had a series of acupuncture treatments, and from a genuine Chinese acupuncturist at that. What made her sure he was genuine was that he was unmistakably Chinese and had to communicate through an interpreter. Also he had to be paid in cash that was wrapped in a piece of paper and thrust into his shirt pocket when he wasn't looking. There was something very Oriental about it all, though she tells me that as she looked around at her fellow patients, studded with needles, she was reminded of portraits of Saint Sebastian.

My wife got temporary relief from this acupuncturist. I think she was relieved that she received no infection from the unsterilized needles. She was also relieved that the place wasn't raided by the state Medical Association.

Arthritis is one of the commonest afflictions of those of us who are getting along in years. I have it myself, in my neck. Sometimes when I am in a public place, such as standing in line at the post office, I forget and turn my head too quickly. The resultant cracking noise can be heard all the way to the mail sorters, and to those not in the know it can be terrifying. They think a supporting beam has broken and the ceiling may cave in. I have a jovial friend who says that when I crack my neck it sounds like a falling tree, and he gets much pleasure out of shouting, "Timber!"

But arthritis isn't so bad. That is, it could be worse. I once hymned it in the following lines:

Arthritis is a dread disease.
It gets you in the wrists and knees.
It gets you in the neck and fingers,
And where it gets you, there it lingers.
Arthritis pains at many points
But mostly settles in the joints.
I rather doubt it ever goes

Into such regions as the nose
Or eyes or lips or even ears,
For which let's offer three small cheers.

Moreover arthritis, painful though it may be, is rarely if ever fatal. I would prefer arthritis to many diseases I could mention but won't.

Both men and women have arthritis, but it seems to me more women have it, or have it worse. This is true in our family, where my wife's arthritis, already mentioned, is more widespread and far more painful than mine. But she (and I think this is true of most women) has a higher threshold of pain or is more stoic or complains less than I would under the same circumstances.

We refer to women as the "weaker sex," but when it comes to some things, such as tolerating pain, I think they are the stronger sex. It seems to me fortunate that women, not men, go through childbirth. All men do is pace the floor while it is going on (or coming out) and wonder whether their insurance will cover the bills. I have heard of men passing out, but usually it was passing out cigars.

Another affliction that is associated with old age, although some youngish people also have it, is insomnia. Perhaps insomnia is something that is most troublesome in middle age and along in the sixties and seventies. When you get into your eighties and nineties, you often get over it.

"How did you sleep last night?" I ask a friend of mine who is eighty-four.

"I slept like a baby," he says. Or sometimes "I slept like a top."

Sleeping like a top has always intrigued me. It must be a dizzying experience. I find it more comforting when my friend says "I slept like a log," which gives me the idea that he had a good night, without a trace of restlessness.

This is not an occasional experience with him. It happens every night, and I have pretty well stopped asking him how he slept. For one thing, I know without asking. For another, I am envious. I am in that slightly earlier time of life when insomnia seems to hit just about everyone. It is a prime topic of conversation, as good as the weather or politics.

A while ago I came upon this fascinating (to me) item in the newspaper: "A glass of port or sherry at bedtime is as good as a sleeping pill." It prompted me to write a piece called "I Can Dream, Can't I?" which I quote herewith:

> This item makes me very merry,
> Encouraging the use of sherry
> Or port, for those who like the taste,
> When with a sleepless night one's faced.
>
> I see now what it is I need
> Along with bedside books I read.
> Before another night shall pass,
> Beside my bed I'll place a glass.

A bottle might be better yet
If sleep is rather hard to get,
Or possibly a gallon jug
If I should need a king-size slug.

Oh, no prescription, smaller cost,
The sense of guilt now all but lost. . . .
I have a thought, though, that's divine:

A water bed that's filled with wine,
With tube attached that, dusk to dawn,
Much like a babe I'd suckle on.

Taking a little drink, or nightcap, before going to bed is suggested by many physicians. But since alcohol is also said to reduce the number of brain cells, one is confronted by a dilemma. To the elderly insomniac, however, the choice is not difficult. There are still plenty of brain cells left to do whatever thinking is required, and a good night's sleep is worth almost any sacrifice.

Recent studies, it is true, have shown that you need less sleep as you get older. In fact there is some doubt that anyone needs to get the proverbial "eight hours" every night. Five or six hours of good, sound sleep would appear to be sufficient for many. Thomas A. Edison slept only briefly, often on a table or desk in his laboratory, with a stack of books for a pillow. His scanty sleep seems not to have hurt him, though his book-pillow may have, since he lived to the ripe age of eighty-four.

The older insomniac, who doesn't have to get to work at a certain hour, has the advantage of being able to stay in bed until nine or ten or whenever he wants to get up. He has the further advantage of being able to take a catnap (not to be confused with catnip) in the mid-morning or after lunch or whenever.

As for those who may not sleep well at night but can take a restful nap any old time, I have known elderly persons who go to sleep in the middle of a conversation. Out of consideration for their age, no one blames them a bit, except the person who at the moment is doing the talking.

Pity the young, the pre-retired, who get nothing more than a coffee break. Moreover, they drink their coffee to keep themselves awake on the job, and not to relax in preparation for a nap.

Arthritis and insomnia are only two of the ailments that accompany age. These, as I have indicated, are excellent topics of conversation. There is one physical trouble, however, about which some have great reluctance to speak. I refer to that problem faced by most males in their sixties or seventies, the enlarged prostate gland.

This is a perfectly normal development, or over-development, and there is no reason for shame or secretiveness about it. Besides, it has been proved that a prostatectomy need not inhibit a man's sex life. Yet I have friends who will not even use the word "prostate" in public, along with those who if they mention it at all speak of their "prostrate" gland. If the gland were indeed prostrate, as well as slender, it would cause no discomfort.

"I've been having a little trouble with my plumbing," say some, using a rather homely, or homey, euphemism.

Others think even that too explicit and merely blush and change the subject. You would think they had had V.D., or at least a vasectomy.

Happily, I travel (rather slowly) in a group of friends who are very frank about their prostate glands. One, who had a prostatectomy when he was in his early seventies, is not only happy to talk about it but proud. It happens to have been the largest prostate gland ever removed in the local hospital.

"It was as big as a grapefruit," he will tell anyone, and his urologist confirms this by saying it was Size 7, which is about as sizable as they come, o being normal. I have been told I have a Size 2, which is large enough to call for occasional treatment but not big enough to be proud of or to dominate the conversation with.

On his birthday, the son and daughter of my friend presented him with a grapefruit wrapped in fancy red paper. On it was inscribed "Daddy's Prostate." He loved it.

Maybe I am a bawdy, latter-day Elizabethan, but I *like* to talk about such earthy, human, universal things. I compare the liver spots on the backs of my hands with those of others my age, and find I can outspot almost anyone. I call attention to my baldness, which saves me the use of a comb and brush. Not having dentures, I am limited to the vicarious pleasure I get from the denture-adhesive commercials on TV. But I have two partial plates, and I think they are a credit to the profession of dentistry. Even though I am what is called a bruxist, grinding my teeth in disconcerting fashion, I know that without these partial plates my chewing surface would be reduced about forty percent. I might still be able to chew the fat, but that's about all.

If I were a woman, I would have no hesitation about mentioning my hysterectomy, which is nothing to get hysterical about. It usually comes, if it comes at all, at an earlier age than a man's prostatectomy, but it is a part of life—a part, fortunately, that can be parted with.

From talking with friends, from watching TV, and from reading the medical columnists, as one grows older one learns more and more about the human anatomy and what can go wrong with it, from respiratory allergies to cardiac edema and from hypertension to gastric hyperacidity. One becomes familiar with remedies ranging from analgesics to diuretics and from antibiotics to tranquilizers.

I propose that everyone reaching the age of ninety, except for those who say "I haven't been sick a day in my life," be given an honorary M.D.

In addition to the sources of medical information I have mentioned, there are of course the annual and perhaps semi-annual checkups as well as increasingly frequent visits to the doctor's office to fix up this or that.

Some of the very elderly perhaps need to visit a specialist in geriatrics, a geriatrician or gerontologist. But most of us will probably continue going to our family physician, and we and our contemporaries are likely to meet in his office.

Frankly, I enjoy such sessions: reading old magazines I had overlooked on my previous visit; sizing up the other patients in the waiting room, both friends and strangers, and diagnosing each of them; looking over the nurses in their immaculate white (and tight-fitting) uniforms; and finally getting the call that I'm next.

I have a copy of my complete physical examination, and I can tell anyone (and often do) my systolic and diastolic blood pressure, my cholesterol count, the ups and downs of my latest electrocardiogram, and what the lab reported about my urine sample. My doctor shines a light into my eyes, looks down my throat, feels my pulse, checks my blood pressure, thumps my chest, listens to my heart, tests my reflexes by hammering me just under the knees, and says "Come back in about three months."

I can hardly wait that long, and usually don't. I may meet a friend in the waiting room and have a chance to compare conditions with him. Besides, I want to hear from the doctor himself, and not just from my know-it-all neighbor, how I am doing. Best of all, I am always glad to get back a little of what I have paid in to the Government, thanks to Medicare.

Young people, who see a doctor only when they have broken a leg skiing or when they have a cold or when they need a new supply of birth-control pills, don't know the pleasure of these frequent visits, the variety of ailments possible, or the supreme satisfaction of walking out with what is called a "clean bill of health."

It isn't the bill that is clean, unless the doctor has had it sterilized before the receptionist hands it to you. You are the clean one, and you feel mighty good about it, at least for a while.

You may even kick up your heels, as you come out of the doctor's office, unless you are afraid of getting your sacroiliac out of whack again.

At the beginning of this chapter I said that what I want most as I grow older is good health. However, there is an optimistic way of looking at illness. It can be put this way, in "When I'm Down I'm Up":

I've TV to watch, I've a book I can read,
I've everything, really, a person could need.
My pillow is patted, my blanket pulled straight.
I'm feeling important, a feeling that's great.
I've flowers, I've letters, I've gifts by the score,
I'm talked to, I'm listened to. Who could ask more?
I sleep undisturbed, and I eat in my bed,
In fact if I want I can even be fed.
My helpers come running at ring of a bell. . . .
I wish I were treated like this when I'm well.

13.

Generating Generations

Someone probably knows, but I don't, what is the earliest instance of childbirth. Theoretically and biologically I am sure it is possible for a girl to have a daughter when she is twelve. If her daughter in turn has a daughter when she is twelve, the first girl, now a young woman, could be a grandmother at twenty-four.

Usually it is in your later years, however, that you are a grandparent or, if everyone starts early enough, a great-grandparent. We did not have our first granddaughter until we were sixty-three and our first grandson until we were sixty-six. To become grandparents in your mid-sixties is fairly normal, though maybe a little on the late side. A few of our contemporaries are great-grandparents, but it looks as if we are going to have to wait a while. Unless, of course, our granddaughter has a baby when she is twelve, which is something we are not encouraging.

If you have to wait until you are along in years to be a grandparent, it is worth it. It really doesn't matter much what you are called. I had thought I might be a respectful "Grandfather" or a familiar "Gramp." But I turned out to be "Gimp." After all, I called my grandmother "Dan Dan," so I guess I had it coming to me.

"Gimp," I have learned, has many meanings, none of which, I hope, has anything to do with being a grandfather. For instance a gimp is "a nun's neckerchief or stomacher," "a silk fishline strengthened with wire," and "a thread coarser than any other in the same piece of lace." It is that coarseness that bothers me a little, but I am sure my granddaughter did not have it in mind when she first called me Gimp. Worst of all, probably, is a gimp nail, which is "a small forged nail with a rounded head." I would swear on a stack of Bibles (if I could find enough Bibles around the house to make a stack) that I have never forged anything. But I must admit that I have a fairly round head, which those who call me either an egghead or a blockhead would do well to remember.

I am really lucky, however, that I am not called Pimp.

But it isn't what one is called that matters. It is just being called.

"Gimp," my granddaughter calls.

"Yes?" I say. She is a small girl and has a small voice, and yet I hear her without difficulty. This again makes me feel that it is not my ears but others' mumbling that causes me to be thought hard of hearing. Perhaps she speaks more distinctly than most. Perhaps, because her vocabulary is limited, she uses no long words that I have difficulty making out. Perhaps I can hear what I want to hear, and I want to hear her.

"Tell me a story, Gimp," she says. I have given up asking her to add "please." It is enough merely to be asked, and to be listened to.

My stories may not be remarkable, but I get rapt, undivided attention. When I finish my story, I know what to expect and am rarely disappointed.

"Tell me another story, Gimp," she says.

So I tell her another story, and another. Or, temporarily running out of stories, I read to her from a book. It hurts me a little to admit it, but many books contain stories better than any I can make up. I think my granddaughter knows this, but she is kind enough to make no invidious comparisons.

The only thing I insist on, when I tell my granddaughter a story or read to her, is that she snuggle up close to me. I like it also when she looks up at me with her big blue eyes, and I can tell she is listening intently, and believing every word. My ego, deflated by other members of the household, is inflated to the bursting point by my granddaughter.

Now and then I do something for her I would do for no one else.

"Take them out, Gimp," she says.

What she is asking, or telling, me to do is to take out my partial plates. I did this a few times, without being asked, when she was very small, and it frightened her. But it is a sign of her maturation, as the educational psychologists would say, that she now thinks it funny for me to take out these tooth-studded pieces of shiny metal. She is still a little incredulous, but then whatever Gimp does, however hard to believe, is authentic.

She has also asked my wife to take out her partial plates, but my wife, a wonderful grandmother in every other way, firmly refuses.

After all, how could she? She hasn't any.

When it comes to partial plates, if nothing else, I have the edge over her. I can hardly wait to get full dentures. They should keep my granddaughter happy for quite a while.

Our grandson, a latecomer, is still too young to be told stories to or read to or shown false teeth. But young as he is, he is, as they say, "all boy." I am glad he is not part boy, no matter how small or large a part.

His forte is strength, muscles, even at a very early age. He likes to wrestle with me, and I like to wrestle with him. He puts me down, pins my shoulders to the floor. At first I let him do it, and lost graciously. But increasingly the tussle is close. Very soon, as he gets stronger and I get weaker, he will put me down fairly and squarely, or at least fairly. And then the time will come when wrestling with me will be no fun, will be too easy, and he will be out looking for someone his size who will give him more of a challenge.

I like a very feminine granddaughter and a very masculine grandson, and, happily, that is what I have got. In fact I just plain like having grandchildren—but what grandparent doesn't?

In an earlier chapter I described how the retired person, with time on his or her hands, loves to travel and to bring home films of distant places and show them to half-asleep or completely asleep friends. Well, you don't have to travel at all to have plenty of pictures to show—if you have grandchildren.

My wallet is so full of pictures of my grandchildren that there is hardly room for my Medicare and Social Security cards, my driver's license, and my credit cards. Lately I have taken to carrying a second wallet, for the overflow.

"Would you like to see some pictures of my grandchildren?" I ask people the first time I meet them.

"Of course! Show them to us," they exclaim with feigned enthusiasm, and out come the pictures, each accompanied by a lengthy explanation.

The only trouble is that I must then look at the pictures of *their* grandchildren and put up as good a show as they did of being impressed by the children's attractiveness, intelligence, and resemblance to one or both of the grandparents.

But it is worth it. Everything about having grandchildren is worth it, and that includes entertaining them when you want to watch your favorite TV show, going with them to the park and being on edge every moment when they are climbing onto the back of the cement dinosaur or sliding down the steep slide or swinging a little too high on the swing, or perhaps when you are taking them to the zoo and walking and walking, from the monkeys to the lions and from the bears to the hippopotamuses when you desperately want to sit down and they want to keep moving and you promised not to let them out of your sight.

Grandchildren, at least until they are adolescents and sometimes even then, listen to you and respect you and love you. Your own children, their parents, have primary responsibility for them, while your responsibility, except for short periods of babysitting, is only secondary. As a grandparent, you have all of the pleasures and few of the pains.

If you have to be a bit elderly to have grandchildren and great-grandchildren, that is a small price to pay, if price it is. I wouldn't give up my grandchildren if by so doing I could be ten years younger or twenty or thirty. They fully compensate for such minor annoyances of old age as the lack of hair on my head, declining vision and hearing, insomnia, the arthritis in my neck, that somewhat enlarged prostate gland, and knowing that I haven't nearly as many years ahead of me as I have behind me.

One of the most satisfying feelings I have these days is having generated (with my wife's help) a second generation (my children) and a third generation (my grandchildren) and having it in the cards or wherever to generate a fourth generation.

If you haven't veneration for age, I hope you at least have veneration for generation.

But that's all for now. I just heard someone calling.

"Gimp, tell me a story."

About the Author

Richard Armour, who describes the later years not only gracefully but, in general, affectionately, knows what he is talking about. He is a grandfather twice over; is retired (if you can call writing for magazines and newspapers, lecturing, and doing two books a year retired); and is the right age to speak from experience about both the advantages and the disadvantages of senior citizenry. We have no intention of revealing what the right age is, but if you read this book carefully you can figure it out for yourself.

He has spent nearly forty years of his life as a college professor at a number of institutions, but is perhaps best known for his light verse and prose excursions in the fields of humor and satire. His published books now total 49, including nearly a dozen for children.